Growing older
Growing wiser

KAREN Y. DAVIS

Growing Older, Growing Wiser
Karen Y. Davis
Published by:
ECS Ministries
PO Box 1028
Dubuque, IA 52004-1028
www.ecsministries.org
First Edition 2007
ISBN 978-1-59387-066-9
Copyright © 2007 ECS Ministries

Printed in the United States of America

In memory of Dr. Ed Harlow
who long ago encouraged me to write,
and who modeled what it means to
"grow old in the Lord."

Acknowledgements

This book began as the outgrowth of a subject I first addressed at a women's conference: "What the Bible Says About Getting Older." Valuable technical help was provided by Dr. Ruth Falk and Dr. Luanne Hurst. Thanks also are due to my husband Bill and to Carol Hudson for helpful input, and to the leadership teams of Woman to Woman Bible Study and the Largo-Seminole Women's Bible Study for their support and encouragement.

Contents

Foreword
Growing Older—
Growing Wiser

N one of us have a choice regarding the first phrase—*Growing Older*—that process began the day we were born. But *Growing Wiser?* Now that's another matter, and an important one at that . . . one that requires us to make choices every day.

In this book, Karen Y. Davis draws on her wealth of experience to provide helpful guidelines on both subjects. As a gifted women's Bible class teacher and popular conference speaker, Karen has interacted with women of all ages and situations. She and her husband Bill have also learned much about the subject as they cared for both sets of parents in their own home until the Lord called them to Himself. And finally she has spent many hours researching the subject, primarily in the Holy Scriptures.

The *AIM* of the book? That the Lord would be glorified in the lives of the readers as we discover:

* where to turn to for guidance in the challenges and trials of aging
* how to continue to be useful servants of our Lord
* that our example can (and indeed should) have an impact on others

Those later years can be filled with new opportunities and be full of wonderful surprises as we enjoy more intimate fellowship with the Lord. In doing so, we will discover that He wants us to keep on bearing fruit for His glory until that day when He calls us into His very presence and we will see Him face to face (Psalm 92:14,15; Isaiah 46:4). May it be our desire to *finish well.*

—GERTRUD I. HARLOW

Introduction

At times, I have contemplated writing a book, only to discover that a perfectly good volume on the same subject has already been written. A. W. Tozer used to caution aspiring writers: "You should never write a book unless you just have to."[1] Why add to the decimation of our forests by cutting down trees and turning them into still another book when one exists that adequately covers the subject? After all, as Ecclesiastes 12:12 says, "Of the making of many books there is no end; and much study is a weariness of the flesh" (KJV).

Then one day I spoke at a women's conference on the subject of "Getting Older." In preparation I discovered that, yes, a number of books on the subject of aging existed, but what did they cover? Some were intended to be humorous and were mostly filled with jokes about the aging process. Some provided financial planning advice for retirement and old age. Some dealt with the adjustment process of living with aging parents. Others were biographical in nature, the personal stories of men and women living with cancer or early-stage Alzheimer's.

What I did *not* find was a careful study of the aging process in the Bible itself. Since the Bible is the textbook of the Christian faith, shouldn't we who claim to be Christians know what it says about getting older?

I grew up in a home where the Bible was neither studied nor believed. Since that time I have come to love the Bible as no other book. I appreciate not only the life-changing wisdom found in its pages, but also the honesty (sometimes painful honesty) with which it portrays the lives of real men and women who came to know God. How did these people in the Bible adjust to the aging process? Why did many of them seem godly in their youth but fall into sin and disgrace in later life? What were the pitfalls? How can I learn from their mistakes?

I have struggled with the aging process. Have you? I am a Christian, and many Pollyanna-type books on aging seem to tell me that we go laughing-all-the-way to the finish line—that there is nothing but joy ahead of us. Believers are not supposed to mind the onslaught of wrinkles or the physical, mental, and social changes that accompany aging. But the fact is, we often do. What attitudes *should* we cultivate? We need a perspective that is neither pessimistic nor unrealistic.

Like the proverb that says, "Give me neither poverty nor riches," we need the balanced treatment of aging found in the Bible. Death is called an enemy (1 Cor. 15:26). Fear of death is an acknowledged reality (Heb. 2:15). Godly people in the pages of Scripture grappled with loss and physical limitations. Yet hope and joy and comfort are repeatedly expressed throughout the Bible. "The path of the righteous is like the light of dawn, that shines brighter and brighter until the full day" (Prov. 4:18).

We do not have to end our lives like King Saul, whose life can best be summed up in his own words: "I have played the fool" (1 Sam. 26:21). We can choose instead to model our lives after the apostle Paul, who was able to write in his last letter: "I have finished the course, I have kept the faith; in the future there is laid up for me the crown of righteousness, which the Lord, the righteous Judge, will award to me on that day; and not only to me, but also to all who have loved His appearing" (2 Tim. 4:7-8).

In the following chapters we will scrutinize the lives of many men and women found in the pages of the Bible. Their lives and their words help explain and illustrate the aging process and the related areas of healing, disease, death, and hope.

Too often the Bible is used for decoration instead of authentication. I myself tend to be a skeptical reader. I am not inclined to believe what I read or hear (especially if it pertains to spiritual truth) unless I can see it for myself in context and verify it.

Unfortunately, even in Christian circles, error and sloppy scholarship abound. For that reason, whenever I teach the Bible or speak at a women's conference, I always encourage those present to follow the discussion with an open Bible. Please take advantage of the Scripture references to complete your own study of these fascinating men and women of the Bible and what they can teach us about how to grow old wisely.

—KAREN Y. DAVIS

PART

1

The Aging Process

There are about 3,000 people mentioned by name in the Bible.

Of those 3,000 we only have enough information to evaluate the lives of about 100 of them.

Of those 100, only about one-third of them finished well.

Of those who failed, most failed in the last half of their life.

—HOWARD HENDRICKS

Good News
/ Bad News

*Do not say, "Why is it that the former
days were better than these?" For it is not
from wisdom that you ask about this.*

—ECCLESIASTES 7:10

Remember when you were twelve years old and you thought that anyone who was thirty was old? Later, when you were about twenty, you probably thought that someone dying at the age of sixty was "old" and had lived a full life. Would you think that way at age sixty?! It is amazing how our perspective can change.

Most of us do not greet the aging process with hilarious joy. For much of my life I have been both healthy and busy, too busy to spend a lot of time thinking about getting older. But one day a friend referred to me for the first time as "an older woman." Surprised, I thought, "Is that how people think of me?" It was not an image I was eager to cultivate. Old people are not exactly revered in our culture. Would I soon be considered out-of-date? Ready to be put out to pasture?

My mother was an attractive woman who, in her youth, modeled hats for Montgomery Ward catalogs. Even as a widow with three young children, she attracted suitors, and she remarried when I was twelve-years-old. My mother also never told anyone her age—in fact, it was only by sneaking into her wallet that we children found out her date of birth, and I am not sure even to this day that the numbers on her driver's license were correct! Yet I understand why she kept her age secret. People tend to place you into constraining categories when they know your age. Their expectations and attitudes change.

Our society gives mixed messages about getting older, and perhaps that has always been the case. Herodotus tells us that some tribes worshiped their elders as gods, and others ate them![1] In the 1700s, people wore gray wigs to make themselves look older and wiser; today, people dye their hair to look younger. Outlooks toward aging continue to fluctuate today.

The Bible anticipates changing attitudes toward the elderly and cautions us to "rise up before the gray headed," to "honor the aged," and *not* to despise our mothers when they are old (Lev. 19:32; Prov. 23:22). Younger men are instructed to be subject to their elders (1 Peter 5:5). Even Timothy, exercising leadership delegated to him by the apostle Paul, was warned not to sharply rebuke an older man, but to appeal to him as a father, and to treat the older women as mothers (1 Tim. 5:1-2).

Whatever attitudes we face, our society will need to adjust to a rising population of people over 65 years of age. In 1940 only 4 percent of the population were 65 or over. By the year 2020, 20 percent will be over 65. And by 2025, it is predicted that the elderly will outnumber teenagers 2 to 1.[2]

In some ways, adjusting to the aging process on the personal level equates to the "good news / bad news" jokes. Remember them? "I had good news and bad news at the airport today. The good news is that the first two pieces of luggage out of the baggage chute were mine. The bad news is that they started out as one piece."

Those of us who have a solid relationship with the Lord should not think that getting older is necessarily bad news. With increased age comes experience, greater wisdom, maturity, and new opportunities. We have had a chance to develop and exercise our spiritual gifts. We know (or should know) who we are and how we function in the Christian community and in the world. We look forward to that heavenly city whose architect and builder is God (Heb. 11:10). As the old chorus reminds us,

This world is not my home; I'm just a-passin' through.
If heaven's not my home, O Lord, what will I do?
The angels beckon me from heaven's open door,
And I don't feel at home in this world any more.

On the other hand, many of us *do* view the changes we face during the aging process as "bad news." In later chapters, we will discuss several aspects of aging that we might think of as bad news. Getting closer to the finish line brings many challenges. Personally, I am not among those who wish to live in the past, nor would I like to turn back the clock. One trip through this world is enough for me. But even for believers, facing increasing limitations and other consequences of getting older is not easy—even if the process is slow and we are given time to adjust to it.

Are you getting older? It is easy to take one of the standard tests. You know you are getting older when Happy Hour is an afternoon nap. You know you are getting older when you are faced with two temptations and you choose the one that will get you home by nine o'clock! One day you realize that the pharmacist knows you by name, or the eye doctor tells you that you need bifocals. Possibly in your case, it is finding out that your favorite childhood toys are now in a museum. For others it is hitting a certain age where the last number is zero—thirty, forty, or fifty. At fifty you realize you are one-half century old!

At some point, you look in the mirror and do not

like what you see. You may never have been thrilled with your looks, but now you are even less happy. Wrinkles "magically" appear. Men may begin to carefully comb their thinning hair over a growing bald spot. You say, "Who is that person staring at me in the mirror?" You look at your spouse and ask yourself, "Who is that old person I am married to?" And, of course, there are changes in your body. Gravity is at work.

Perhaps you have started to ask yourself, "Should I dye my hair? What about getting a facelift or using Botox to get rid of these wrinkles on my forehead?" You take more notice of advertisements about mysterious potions, laser treatments, or expensive cosmetics that make extravagant promises, and you ask: Should I get into all that stuff? Is it right? Would God approve? Does He have an opinion about such things?

When we have mixed feelings (or even negative feelings) about getting older, there is no better place to go for answers than the Bible with its timeless wisdom. As it turns out, our God, the Ancient of Days, has much to say on the subject.

For Further Thought . . .

1. Do you see yourself as young, middle-aged, or elderly? How has your perspective on aging changed in the last fifteen years?

2. What attitudes toward the elderly have you observed in society? In the church?

3. Are you comfortable sharing your age with other people? Why or why not?

4. Would you like to turn back the clock to a time when you were younger? Give some reasons for your answer.

5. What are several benefits that go along with your present stage in life.

6. If money were no object, would you consider getting a facelift or some other form of plastic surgery to minimize the appearance of aging? On what basis would you make that decision?

The Purpose of the Aging Process

LORD, remind me how brief my time on earth will be. Remind me that my days are numbered, and that my life is fleeing away.

—PSALM 39:4, NLT

One question that challenges evolutionists is: Why do we age? As the authors of a *Scientific American* book on aging wrote:

How can a phenomenon—aging—that reduces survival and fecundity, and hence reduces evolutionary fitness, result from evolution? Why have the bad genes that cause aging not been weeded out of populations by natural selection? This paradox has intrigued biologists for over a century and has led to a number of creative attempts at its resolution.[1]

While it is not the purpose of this book to discuss scientific theories of how and why we

21

age, it is interesting to read comments like the following in a *Scientific American* article: "The living machines we call bodies were not *designed* for extended operation"[2] (italics added). That fact has not stopped humanity from trying to slow down the aging process for thousands of years.

As far back as the Gilgamesh Epic (about 3000 BC), people have been attempting—unsuccessfully—to defeat aging and death.[3] An Egyptian papyrus from 1600 BC gave instructions for preparing an ointment that would, supposedly, transform an old man into a youth of twenty.[4] In the early 1500s, Ponce de Leon searched in vain for a miraculous Fountain of Youth. Others with a more scientific bent, like Benjamin Franklin, believed the advance of science would inevitably lead to increased longevity. Yet the aging process continues unabated.

It is normal for Christians to wonder why God, who is said to be "the author of every good and perfect gift," has given us the "gift" of aging. In God's original plan, there was no death. God created a world of beauty and fruitfulness and made it all accessible to Adam and Eve. Only one restriction was placed on this bounty: They were forbidden to eat the fruit of one tree. If they did so, God said that they would "surely die" (Gen. 2:17).

If sin had not entered the world, people would have lived forever. But sin brought the penalty of both physical and spiritual death, and death spread to all creation. When Adam and Eve chose to eat of the forbidden fruit, the process of decay and death began to affect the world with shattering implications. Most people do not begin to appreciate how much suffering lies beneath the smiling face of nature. We can hardly imagine the ecology of a world without death.

Some day, as we read in Romans chapter 8, the creation will be set free from its slavery to corruption. We look forward to a re-created world of the future where

> "the wolf will dwell with the lamb . . . Also the cow and the bear will graze, their young will lie down together; and the lion will eat straw like the ox. And the nursing child will play by the hole of the cobra, and the weaned child will put his hand on the viper's den. They will not hurt or destroy in all My holy mountain, for the earth will be full of the knowledge of the LORD as the waters cover the sea" (Isaiah 11:5-9).

Until that time, however, death and dying are a part of God's plan for our lives.

In the book of Genesis, we read that before the flood people lived for hundreds of years. There is no real reason to doubt the accuracy of those numbers. The Bible tells us that Adam lived for 930 years. He lived to see not only his grandchildren, but his great, great, great, great, great, great-grandchildren (eight generations). The entire process of maturing and aging was obviously slower then. Many did not have their first child until the age of seventy or ninety (Gen. 5:9-13).

There may be many reasons for that longevity which we do not understand, but I can think of at least three. First, the world was young, and there had not been time for harmful mutations to accumulate that would increasingly affect the gene pool over time and shorten life. Second, in the early ages of the world, God designed each person to live long enough to be able to pass along the history of the human race to several generations. Before writing was invented, if we had not had such a long oral history, much of what we know from the earliest chapters of Genesis would have been lost to us. Third, we know little about the environment of the world at that early time. It was apparently much more conducive to longevity because after the flood the human lifespan began to diminish dramatically.

By the time of Abraham (approximately 2000 BC), the human lifespan was uniformly less than two hundred years, and by the time of King David (about 1000 BC), people generally were living only to seventy or eighty years, much like today. According to Psalm 90:10, "As for the days of our life, they contain seventy years, or if due to strength, eighty years." Some consider this the optimal age. By age seventy or eighty, we have had enough time to mature and reach our full potential without becoming inflexible and set in our ways. Those who have become experts at doing evil are also removed from the scene before they can do even more damage.

Of course, God could have chosen to end our lives when we were feeling our best, at the prime of life. Suppose He had allowed us to live seventy or eighty years, but during that time no visible signs of aging appeared—no wrinkles, no health problems, no tiredness. Why does He allow deterioration to take place in our bodies before we die?

For many of us, it is hard to set our affection on things above when the world is so much with us. We all tend to cling to life with both hands. We are apt to put off thinking about the hereafter unless God finds ways to remind us that we are destined for more than this earth. As the aging process begins, He starts to unclench our fists, helping us loosen our grip on life. He turns our hearts toward home—our real home.

Even as we are adjusting to diminished abilities, God is preparing our children and our loved ones for our departure, showing them that they need to take up the slack because we will not always be here. Through our illnesses and shrinking capacities, God is also teaching us new lessons in humility and dependency, conforming us to the image of His Son. At the same time, He is building qualities of unselfishness, patience, and compassion in those left behind who will need to provide for us and care for us in our last days.

We have little choice about the aging process and how soon or how late it will affect us. We do have a choice about how to respond to it.

For Further Thought . . .

1. God is, according to James 1:17, the author of "every good and perfect gift," Do you think of aging as a "gift" from God? Discuss why or why not.

2. How does the aging process foster humility? What are the spiritual advantages of this? See Philippians 2:5-8 and 1 Peter 5:5-6.

3. Observe the genealogies in Genesis chapter 5. How old was Adam when his son Seth was born? Why do you think procreation came so late in life before the Flood?

4. Who in chapter 5 lived longer than any other man? How old was he when his first son was born? How old was he when he died?

5. At your present age, how much time do you spend thinking about heaven? Have you ever made a study of what heaven is really like, who will be there, and what they will be doing?

6. Have you ever been a caregiver for an elderly friend or relative? What were the benefits *for you*?

7. Study the closing words of Jesus in the Sermon on the Mount from Matthew 7:21-28.

    a. What do you learn about heaven in those verses?

    b. What does it mean to "build your house" on a rock, as opposed to sand? See Mathew 7:24-27.

Some People
in the Bible and
How They Aged

Abraham breathed his last and died in a ripe
old age, an old man and satisfied with life.

—GENESIS 25:8

I t is both instructive and comforting to
observe the aging process in the lives of men
and women of the Bible. It is instructive
because we can see how these role models
from long ago handled old age physically,
mentally, and spiritually. Some, like the
patriarch **Joseph**, lived long and ended
gloriously in spite of difficult trials and
hardships. Some lived their early lives in
incredible evil but turned to God late in life.
King Manasseh stands as such an example,
unquestionably the most wicked king Israel
ever had. Although Manasseh could never
undo the evil consequences the nation reaped
because of him, he nevertheless turned to God

in humility and repentance late in life. Others, such as **Gideon,** exhibited great faith and were used mightily by the Lord for a time, but lost spiritual ground in later life (see the end of his story in Judges 8:22-32). As we carefully observe such examples, hopefully we can avoid some of the same pitfalls and temptations that we may be particularly prone to later in life.

Studying the lives of these people is also comforting because we realize that we are not alone. Even good and godly people in the pages of Scripture exhibited signs of aging. They did not necessarily develop various ailments because of sin in their lives, as some people will tell you.[1]

When we think of a godly man who nevertheless had the normal, physical problems of aging in later life, **David, King of Israel,** comes first to mind. God speaks of him as a man after His own heart (Acts 13:22). David experienced a hard life; he was a warrior and had seen many battles. The end of his life is described in 1 Kings, chapters 1 and 2. At that time David was said to be "old, advanced in age." Yet this good man, beloved of God, was obviously not in good health. Although they covered him with blankets, he could not keep warm. When blankets did not work, they hired a beautiful young woman named Abishag to be his hot water bottle and his nurse. The Bible records that David did not cohabit with her. We are not told what specifically was wrong with David. Quite possibly he was suffering with circulatory problems or congestive heart failure, either of which could have produced such symptoms. In any case, he was said to be "advanced in age" at the time, and he died at the age of seventy (2 Sam. 5:4).

Women in the Bible as well as men showed signs of aging. In Genesis 18 we find **Sarah, the wife of Abraham**, "old, advanced in age." At the time she was not only barren, but, as it is rather quaintly put in the King James Version, "It ceased to be with Sarah after the manner of women" (Gen. 18:11). In other words, she was past childbearing and had gone through menopause. If you are struggling with the symptoms of menopause, isn't it comforting to know that you are not the first? This lovely, spirited woman, held up to us as a role model in 1 Peter 3, probably had hot flashes and night sweats. She has been there before you.

Amazingly, on that occasion in Genesis 18, God announced that He planned to do a miracle. Within one year, Abraham and Sarah would have a son. Sarah's response is intriguing. The Bible says that she laughed within herself, saying, "After I have become old, shall I have pleasure, my lord being old also?" It is interesting to speculate on what she meant by *pleasure*. Was she missing having sexual relations with Abraham at the time? Perhaps by this time Sarah had her own tent (Gen. 24:67). When the Bible says that "by faith" Sarah received the ability to conceive (Heb. 11:11), it certainly must have involved once again sharing Abraham's tent and resuming marital relations with him in her old age. Thus at the age of ninety Sarah gave birth to a son, a miracle child named Isaac.

Isaac, that miracle son of Abraham and Sarah, also experienced infirmity in old age. Convinced that he would die soon, Isaac called his favorite son, Esau, and asked him to go hunting and to prepare a savory dish of whatever he caught for Isaac's last meal. At the time, Isaac was old and his eyes were so weak that he could not see. Was it illness or was it depression that made him think he would die soon? Ironically, Isaac actually lived another forty-three years!

When my mother-in-law was in her fifties, she would often say, "I'll never make old bones," yet she lived, in fact, to be ninety-three. What is it that makes some people think they will die sooner than they actually do? In some cases, it may be the pessimistic thinking that accompanies depression. In other cases, it may be because their own fathers or mothers died at a certain age. The Bible, however, instructs us that "No one has power over the day of his death" (Eccl. 8:8 NIV).

Not only Isaac but also his wife **Rebekah** appears to be depressed when we read about her in Genesis 27. She was dealing with a blind husband. She also was dealing with adult twin sons who had numerous character defects and did not get along. To top it off, she had daughter-in-law trouble. In Genesis 27:46

she said, "I am tired of living because of the daughters of Heth" (whom her son Esau had married). She went on to say that if Jacob were to take a wife like them, "What good will my life be to me?" Old age is not without problems, and one of them may be a tendency toward depression.

We can observe the gradual nature of the aging process in **Eli, the priest,** who served at the tabernacle of the Lord in Shiloh during the period of the judges. Notice the clues to his deteriorating health that we see in the first four chapters of 1 Samuel. In chapter 1 we find him sitting by the doorpost of the tabernacle observing Hannah (1:9, 12). She was in distress and praying, and he was watching her mouth. Since he could see her mouth, obviously his eyesight was intact at the time.

In chapter 2 we are told that Eli was "very old" (2:22). Perhaps poor health contributed to his passive attitude toward the outrageous conduct of his adult sons. In chapter 3 we learn that Eli's eyesight had begun to deteriorate and he could not see well (3:2). Finally, in chapter 4 we find Eli sitting once again. He was ninety-eight-years-old, and the Bible tells us that his eyes were "set" so that he could not see. In other words, he was blind (4:13-15). It seems likely that he developed cataracts over a period of time and that they eventually resulted in blindness. Our last view of Eli is of him falling backward off his seat and breaking his neck. The Bible adds this detail: he was very fat (4:18).

For some people, thinning hair or the first few gray hairs which appear announce that the aging process has begun. If that is your experience, you are not alone! The prophet **Samuel** had gray hair (1 Sam. 12:2), **Jacob** had gray hair (Gen. 42:38), and **Elisha** the prophet was bald (2 Kings 2:23).

Barzillai was a friend and ally of King David. He supported David when David's son Absalom rebelled and instigated a coup against his father. You can read about Barzillai in 2 Samuel 17-19. When David once again regained the kingdom, he wanted to repay Barzillai. He invited him to return with him to Jerusalem, where David promised to take care of his needs for the rest of his life. Barzillai graciously declined, saying that at his age (which was eighty), food and drink were wasted on him, since he could not readily taste what he ate or drank, nor could he hear the voices of singers any longer (2 Sam. 19:32-35). Here, in this God-fearing man, we see evidence of diminished ability to hear and to taste food, both of which are common problems of old age.

Let's complete our survey of some of the physical aspects of the aging process in the Bible with two encouraging examples: Caleb and Moses. **Caleb** was a man who followed the Lord fully, as the Bible states on at least three occasions. At age forty he was sent as a spy into the Promised Land to survey it and to bring back a report. Forty-five years later, at age eighty-five, he stated, "I am still as strong today as I was in the day Moses sent me; as my strength was then, so my strength is now, for war and for going out and coming in" (Josh. 14:11). Caleb inherited the territory in Israel now known as Hebron, and he successfully drove out the enemy peoples who lived there.

Our final example, **Moses,** lived to the ripe old age of 120, having spent the previous forty years serving God's people. Up until the time of his death, "his eyes were not dim, nor his natural vigor diminished" (Deut. 34:7). All things are possible!

One is reminded of other vigorous men in more recent times, like George Müller, who began evangelistic tours at the age of seventy. For the next seventeen to eighteen years he traveled the equivalent of eight times around the world. During that time and beyond, until past the age of ninety, he continued to administer many of the responsibilities of the orphanages he had founded. John Wesley was similarly vigorous. At eighty-three he was annoyed that he could not write more than fifteen hours a day without hurting his eyes. At eighty-six he was ashamed he could not preach more than twice a day. He complained in his diary that he had an increasing tendency to lie in bed until five-thirty in the morning!

Whether we remain healthy and vigorous into advanced old age or experience severe limitations before that time, God has provided examples in the Bible to encourage us (and in some cases to *warn* us) along the way. We are not facing some new and strange disorder called "aging" that they did not face. Aging has not taken God by surprise; it need not take us by surprise either. Success is possible. "Therefore we do not lose heart, but though our outer man is decaying, yet our inner man is being renewed day by day" (2 Cor. 4:16).

For Further Thought . . .

1. Several characters in the Bible show evidence of depression later in life. Study Naomi's life in Ruth 1.

    a. Why was she depressed? Why did she believe that the hand of the Lord was against her (1:13)?

    b. What blessings still lay ahead for her in God's plan (4:9-22)?

2. The apostle Paul wrote of his infirmities both in Galatians 4:13-15 and 2 Corinthians 12.

    a. How did God use these afflictions for a good purpose?

    b. What did Paul mean when he stated, "When I am weak, then I am strong" (2 Cor. 12:10)?

3. Name several people you know who have been positive role models of growing older. List some of the characteristics or attributes about them that you appreciate.

4. We do not usually welcome the first signs of aging, such as gray hair. How does the Bible view the significance of this early evidence of getting older? See Leviticus 19:32.

5. Samson's life was filled with rebellion and disobedience. His last days were spent in a Philistine prison, blinded, mocked, and abused. He could have easily given up, believing there was nothing he could accomplish for God. Read of his final moments in Judges 16:23-30. See what is said about him in Hebrews 11:32-34.

What Is Happening to My Body?

If wrinkles must be written upon our brows,
let them not be written upon the heart.

—PRESIDENT JAMES A. GARFIELD

It surprises some people to learn that God not only gives examples of the aging process in people of the Bible, but even describes the aging process itself in Ecclesiastes 12, which begins with these words:

"Remember also your Creator in the days of your youth, before the evil days come and the years draw near when you will say, 'I have no delight in them.' "

Believers are happy to stress this first part of that verse; "Remember your Creator in the days of your youth." That is the optimal time for learning, for building good habits, for memorizing Scripture, for laying a good spiritual foundation for life. But we tend to shy away from the last part of the verse: ". . .

before the *evil days* come and the years draw near when you will say, 'I have *no delight* in them'" (italics added). We Christians, as well as our society, often refuse to look realistically at such a time.

Of course, the Hebrew word for *evil* there does not necessarily imply moral evil. It is a word commonly used for adversity, affliction, or trouble. Afflictions may come, and natural and physical pleasures may decline, but spiritually, it is possible to be in the best shape of our lives.

I live in Florida, land of the golden retirement years. Periodicals for seniors abound, and the articles tend to be uniformly cheerful. (Would people read them if they weren't?) We see pictures of men in their eighties running a marathon or flying along on waterskis; women in their eighties and even nineties dancing, swimming, taking classes, or bungee jumping. I was feeling rather smug and pleased with myself when, as an "older woman," I began working out at a gym. Then I learned that many women who participate in such programs are far older than me! One is in her mid-eighties. And women as old as ninety-nine attend Bible classes I teach.

Yes, it is true. Your health, your energy, your mind, and your activities *may* survive well into your eighties or nineties. However, that is not the typical pattern. Hidden among the cheery articles in such well-meaning periodicals are advertisements on each page for assisted living facilities, nursing homes, wheelchair accessories, incontinence supplies, and so on. The Bible is realistic about growing older, and I believe God wants us to be, too.

Susanna Wesley must have been thinking about the opening verses of Ecclesiastes 12 when she wrote this letter to her son:

> Believe me, my dear son, old age is the worst time we can choose to mend either our lives or our fortunes. If the foundations of solid piety are not laid early in sound principles and virtuous disposition; if we neglect, while strength and vigor last, to lay up something before the infirmities of old age overtake us—it is an hundred to one odds, that we shall die both poor and wicked.[1]

Ecclesiastes 12:2, continuing with its portrayal of aging, describes a time when the sun, the light, the moon, and the stars are darkened, and clouds return after the rain. It is a picture of gathering storm clouds and the fading capacity for joy. Some suggest that the cloudy weather implies mental sluggishness or the beginnings of senility.[2] In that day, Solomon poetically continues:

> "The keepers of the house tremble, and the mighty men stoop; the grinding ones stand idle because they are few, and those who look through windows grow dim" (12:3).

Here he compares the body to an old house, reminding us of the apostle Paul's words in 2 Corinthians 5:1: "If the earthly tent which is our house is torn down, we have a building from God, a house not made with hands, eternal in the heavens." The symbolism of Ecclesiastes 12 is not hard to discern. *The keepers* (guardians, watchmen) of the house are the arms—our first line of defense or protection. With age they become less steady; they may tremble with palsy (paralysis). *The mighty men* are our thighs and legs which support the bulk of our weight. They may stoop and give rise to a characteristic shuffle in old age. *The grinding ones* are teeth, few in number, or missing, in the absence of conscientious dental work! And *those who look through the windows*, our eyes, grow dim. Most people experience some deterioration in their vision in later years. Hearing may also diminish with old age:

"... and the doors on the street are shut, as the sound of the grinding mill is low, and one will arise at the sound of the bird, and all the daughters of song will sing softly" (12:4).

Even in the absence of hearing aids, elderly people can "shut the doors on the street." They can stop listening to the world around them because the sounds are indistinct and take too much effort to decipher. At other times, little sounds may seem loud to them, like the tap-tap of a woodpecker at six o'clock in the morning. With old age comes wakefulness and disturbed patterns of sleep: They rise up at the sound of a bird!

The aging process affects both our ability to hear music and to produce it. When Solomon states that "all the daughters of song will sing softly," he may be referring to the inability to hear music (audiologists tell us that hearing loss begins with the high notes) or to produce music because of changes in our vocal cords which affect the volume and quality of our singing. Verse 5 continues:

> "Furthermore, men are afraid of a high place and of terrors on the road; the almond tree blossoms, the grasshopper drags himself along, and the caperberry is ineffective. For man goes to his eternal home while mourners go about in the street."

My older brother enjoyed climbing water towers for fun in his youth. Heights meant nothing to him. Many of us loved the thrill of a good roller coaster ride in our twenties or thirties. Later years, however, can produce lack of balance and fear of stumbling. We become afraid of high places and terrors on the road. Reflexes slow; reaction time lengthens. There is a tendency to become more fearful, knowing that we can no longer protect ourselves as readily as we once could. We stick to the back roads and no longer feel competent to battle eight lanes of traffic at rush hour or on a rainy night.

Still other symptoms appear: *The almond tree blossoms*. Almond trees produce white blossoms in the spring, suggesting hair that turns white with old age. Solomon next speaks of the grasshopper dragging himself along. One can picture the uncoordinated gait of those whose infirmities cause them to move slowly and awkwardly.

And finally, even *the caperberry is ineffective* (12:5, NASB, Darby).[3] The caperberry was thought to be the Viagra of the day; it was supposed to stimulate sexual desire. But Solomon pictures a time when such remedies are futile.

Scholars do not agree on the precise meaning of the images found in verse 6:

> "Remember Him before the silver cord is broken and the golden bowl is crushed, the pitcher by the well is shattered, and the wheel at the cistern is crushed."

Whether the golden bowl refers to the brain or to the preciousness of life is less important than seeing that the verbs (broken, crushed, shattered) imply the cessation of life. Whether by heart attack, stroke, or other means, life on earth comes to an end. "It is the same for all. There is one fate [death] for the righteous and for the wicked; for the good, for the clean, and for the unclean" (Eccl. 9:2). At that time, Solomon concludes, "The dust will return to the earth" (Eccl. 12:7a).

Why does God, through King Solomon, give us these details about how the aging process takes place? Certainly not just to depress us. The extensive description of what happens to our bodies as we age strips away delusive attitudes and our tendency to close our eyes to unpleasant realities. Unfortunately, today those attitudes are found not just in society as a whole but even in the professing church.

We have a sampler hanging on the wall in our home which has been passed down through our family for generations. It was done by a relative of Sir Francis Drake named Mary Ann Drake. According to what is written on the sampler, she stitched it at the age of ten, completing it on March 2, 1819. Embroidered on the sampler are these words:

> *Fragrant the rose is, but it fades in time,*
> *The violet sweet, but quickly past the prime.*
> *White lilies hang their heads and soon decay,*
> *And whiter snow in minutes melts away.*
> *Such and so with'ring are our early joys*
> *Which time or sickness speedily destroy.*

It is interesting to observe the reactions of visitors who approach the sampler near enough to read the words. "How morbid!" I sometimes hear. "Why on earth would they teach a child such a depressing verse?"

Solomon's words—and Mary Ann Drake's sampler—remind us that we must have something to replace all the things which gradually (or suddenly) are taken away. God intends that void to be replaced with Himself. Nothing else will do. When all is said and done, "The spirit will return to God who gave it" (Eccl. 12:7b). We need to be prepared for that time.

For Further Thought . . .

1. Why do you think we are told to remember our Creator *in the days of our youth* (Eccl. 12:1)? What are the advantages of that? What about those who come to know the Lord late in life?

2. Solomon speaks of a time when "the evil days come and the years draw near when you will say, 'I have *no delight* in them'" (Eccl. 12:1). What is your reaction to that statement? Is it still possible to have joy at such a time? What is the difference between *delight* and *joy*?

3. What hope did Old Testament believers have for continued existence after death (Eccl. 12:7; Ps. 71:20; 73:24; 23:6)?

4. What habits of life are apt to cause people to die sooner? Live longer? See Proverbs 10:27; 3:1-2; 4:10; 9:10-11; and Ephesians 6:1-3. Are there exceptions to these principles? Read and comment on Psalm 73.

5. Well-established statistics indicate that people of faith tend to live longer. Why do you think this might be true?

6. Are there compensations for the physical disabilities that come with old age? Name some.

Aging Role Models
—Good and Bad

Making Hard Choices:
Paul, Abraham, Moses

*Those that are bound for heaven must be
willing to swim against the stream, and must
not do as the most do, but as the best do.*

—MATTHEW HENRY

The Bible often pictures the Christian life as a race, yet never as a hundred-yard dash. It is not how we begin the race but how we end it that matters most. There are approximately 3,000 people whose names are listed in the Bible. We have only enough information to evaluate the lives of about one hundred of them. Unfortunately, of those one hundred, only about one-third finished well. And when we look at the lives of those who failed, most failed in the last half of their lives.[1]

What can we learn from those who finished well? We tend to focus on good role models, and so we should. Later, though, we will consider what we also can learn from those who failed or who took a downward turn in their latter years. But first, the book of Hebrews gives prerequisites for what constitutes a good role model: "Remember those who led you, who spoke the word of God to you, *and considering the outcome of their conduct*, imitate their faith" (Heb. 13:7, italics added). In another place we are reminded not to be lazy "but imitators of those who *through faith and patience* inherit the promises" (Heb. 6:12, italics added).

At least four times **the apostle Paul** urged believers to follow him as an example (2 Thess. 3:7, 9; 1 Cor. 4:16; 11:1). He never claimed to be perfect. He pressed on to know Christ more fully, yet he also realized that we can benefit from observing the lives of role models who have gone on before us. We don't know how old Paul was at the end of his life, but in his letter to Philemon he described himself as "Paul, the aged" (1:9). In his last letter he knew that the end was near. He wrote, "I have fought the good fight, I have finished the course, I have kept the faith" (2 Tim. 4:7).

Paul was also a man with physical disabilities. Scholars have speculated about the nature of Paul's physical problems. In his letter to the Galatians he spoke of a bodily illness which was apparently disfiguring or unsightly. He was aware that it might have caused the Galatian believers to despise or loathe him (Gal. 4:13-14). To the Corinthians he wrote of his "thorn in the flesh," an infirmity he prayed God would heal. God, however, chose not to heal him, and Paul accepted God's verdict, recognizing that He had a purpose for it. He wrote words which we too would do well to remember as we are getting older:

> "I am well content with weaknesses, with insults, with distresses, with persecutions, with difficulties, for Christ's sake; for when I am weak, then I am strong" (2 Cor. 12:10).

Paul, who ministered in spite of physical problems that might have caused a lesser man to remain out of the spotlight, inspires us to stay in the race even when we have disfiguring or embarrassing physical problems that would make it easy for us to remain on the sidelines.

Abraham, that great man of faith, was told by God to leave his country and go to a land that God would show him. As the book of Hebrews expresses it, "He went out, not knowing where he was going" (Heb. 11:8). At the time Abraham left Mesopotamia, he was seventy-five-years-old.[2] We admire Abraham for many reasons, but we often overlook the first step of faith he took—leaving his native city, Ur of the

Chaldeans. Today the city of Ur, located in southern Iraq, has been extensively excavated. We know that Abraham did not leave some small country town. Ur was a cosmopolitan city with paved streets, schools, and two-story houses containing interior courtyards elaborately paved with mosaic tile.[3]

Many of us would be inclined to balk if God directed us to move to another city. (*Would we argue with God? Doubt His leading?*) Imagine being told to leave not as a young person just starting out in life but as someone established in the community. Imagine God then instructing you to leave before knowing your destination! Imagine being sent to an unknown place in an unknown country that only later would be revealed to you.

Abraham is a role model for many reasons. A man of enormous faith, he made hard choices to follow God. In this instance, Abraham stands out for not allowing his lifestyle or his possessions to possess him. He was willing to accept change. When it is time to downsize in later life, or to move to a new place at such a time, remember the example of Abraham.

Perhaps the power of example is nowhere more evident than in the life of **Moses**. This servant of God began life in difficult circumstances. Orders had come from the king of Egypt to kill all male babies born to the Israelites. Imagine the terror of his godly parents as they attempted to conceal a crying baby from the king's spies. No wonder not only Moses, but also his parents are listed among the heroes of faith in Hebrews chapter 11. They hid him for three months, and "they were not afraid of the king's edict" (11:23). When Moses' parents could conceal him no longer, they put Moses in a carefully prepared basket and placed it in the reeds of the Nile River near where the daughter of Pharaoh came to bathe.

You no doubt remember the story of his rescue, and how, in the kindness of God, Moses' own mother was summoned to be his nurse. Raised in Pharaoh's household, Moses could easily have rejected his heritage, abandoned his people, and settled down to a life of ease in the palace. But we read these words about him in Hebrews 11:24-26:

> "By faith Moses, when he had grown up, refused to be called the son of Pharaoh's daughter; choosing rather to endure ill-treatment with the people of God than to enjoy the passing pleasures of sin, considering the reproach of Christ greater riches than the treasures of Egypt; for he was looking to the reward."

When we make hard choices for God, circumstances do not necessarily improve; in fact, they sometimes get worse. When Moses saw an Egyptian mistreating a fellow Israelite, he killed the Egyptian and buried him in the sand. Moses, the murderer!—not exactly the picture we envision for one of the future great role models of the Bible.

Moses fled. Can you imagine his feelings at such a time? He was about forty years old when his vision of bringing about deliverance for the Israelites crumbled to dust. How could he expect that God would ever use him again? What did Moses think, as ten, twenty, thirty years went by? Finally, when forty years had passed, and Moses was now eighty (Acts 7:22-30), God spoke to him and called him to lead His people out of Egypt and into the Promised Land. By that time Moses had lost all self-confidence (probably exactly what God intended).

The experiences that Moses had with God throughout his life are beyond what we can readily imagine. He *saw* the God of Israel. He heard His voice. His face shone with reflected glory after spending time in God's presence.[4] At one point, the Lord had this to say about Moses:

> "Hear now My words: If there is a prophet among you, I, the LORD, shall make Myself known to him in a vision. I shall speak with him in a dream. Not so with My servant Moses; He is faithful in all My household; with him I speak mouth to mouth, even openly, and not in dark sayings, and he beholds the form of the LORD" (Num. 12:6-8).

Moses was indeed faithful. Through the difficult and degrading experiences of his life, he became "very humble, more than any man who was on the face of the earth" (Num. 12:3). God could trust

Moses with His glory. For forty years in the wilderness, Moses put up with a generation of people who continually challenged his leadership and rebelled against God. Yet when he died at the age of 120, this man was so highly esteemed by the people of Israel that the entire nation mourned and wept for him for thirty days.

What lessons emerge from the life of this godly man? Are you called upon to leave the privileges of a pampered lifestyle to serve the Lord in a hard place? Moses chose "rather to endure ill-treatment with the people of God than to enjoy the passing pleasures of sin" (Heb. 11:25). Do you fear that the wrong choices made early in life will prevent you from ever being used by God again? Think of Moses and find encouragement. Do you become exasperated with the low level of spirituality among those whom God has called you to serve? Remember the attitude of Moses who, in the presence of rebellious people, was "more humble than any man on the face of the earth." Moses inspires us not to give up. His example reminds us not to be satisfied with a superficial knowledge of God, but to go deeper and seek to know God in all His glory to the very end of our days.

For Further Thought . . .

1. Name some other hard choices that the apostle Paul made to follow God. See, for example, his choice not to bribe the governor Felix—a choice which cost Paul two more years in jail (Acts 24:24-27).

2. What are some qualities that are important in choosing a role model? Whom would you ask to mentor you, or to whom would you go for spiritual advice?

3. List several ways in which Moses functioned as a meaningful role model.

4. Were you ever deeply disillusioned by someone who had been a role model for you but who later disappointed you? What did you learn from that experience?

5. Study the hard choice that Abraham was called on to make in Genesis 22. What promise of God did Abraham take into consideration in making that choice? (Heb. 11:17-19)

Overcoming Obstacles:
Joseph, Sarah, Daniel

Must I be carried to the skies on flow'ry beds of ease,
While others fought to win the prize and sailed
through bloody seas?

—Isaac Watts

J oseph, great-grandson of Abraham and Sarah, grew up in what today would be considered a highly dysfunctional family. Conflict and jealousy abounded between his father's wives and between Joseph and his brothers. His sister Dinah had been raped, and two of his brothers, Simeon and Levi, had gone on a murderous rampage that made it necessary for the family to relocate to another city in Canaan. To compound Joseph's problems, his father showed blatant favoritism toward him, which caused his brothers to envy and despise him.

The situation came to a head one day when Joseph's father sent him to check on the welfare of his brothers who were tending the flocks. His brothers saw him coming and conspired to kill him. They threw him into a pit and then coolly sat down to eat their lunch. Although Joseph pleaded with them, and they saw the anguish of his soul, they showed no mercy (Gen. 42:21). When a caravan of Ishmaelites passed by headed for Egypt, Joseph's brothers hauled him out of the pit and sold him to them as a slave. The brothers returned home with the story that Joseph had been killed by a wild animal.

Years went by and Joseph survived. He faced obstacles (such as serving time in prison for a crime he did not do) that few of us are called on to face. By the grace of God he rose in fame and fortune to become one of the two most powerful men in the land of Egypt. The time came when his brothers (who no longer recognized him) stood before him seeking to buy grain. Now was Joseph's perfect opportunity for revenge.

But you probably know the rest of the story. Instead of exhibiting bitterness and revenge, Joseph pursued reconciliation with his brothers. He had had years to sit and remember the wrongs he had undergone at the hands of his family in his youth. How easily he could have become "a bitter old man." Yet with utmost sincerity he reassured his brothers, "As for you, you meant evil against me, but God meant it for good" (Gen. 50:20).

Why is Joseph an important role model? We could list many things, but his willingness to forgive shines out preeminently. Not long ago I heard a woman say about her own father: "He is becoming a bitter old man." What about us? Do we play games, pretending to forgive those who wronged us years ago (because Christians are *supposed* to forgive) while holding deep grudges against them? Are we still angry at heart and alienated from old friends and relatives? Does God bring a name or a face to your mind whom you have never truly forgiven?

On one occasion I heard an older woman say, "Once somebody has crossed me, they're out of my life and thoughts." Such an attitude not only grieves the Holy Spirit but also produces a life of loneliness with few, if any, friends. When the Lord Jesus taught His disciples to pray, He included the words, "And forgive us our debts, as we also have forgiven our debtors" (Matt. 6:12). He ended His instruction on prayer with these solemn words:

> "For if you forgive others for their transgressions, your heavenly Father will also forgive you. But if you do not forgive others, then your Father will not forgive your transgressions" (Matt. 6:14-15).

We have already considered **Sarah, the wife of Abraham,** as an example of how people in the Bible aged, but we would be remiss if we did not also consider her as one of the great role models of Scripture. The apostle Peter mentions Sarah as one of the "holy women" of former times who exhibited a "gentle and quiet spirit" and was submissive to her own husband. Wives are entitled to be called "her children," Peter writes, "if you do what is right without being frightened by any fear" (1 Pet. 3:4-6).

When you study Sarah's life, however, it seems remarkable at first that she would be touted as a role model. She was, after all, no shrinking violet, and she did not always do what was right. She was a woman of strong character who at times argued with her husband. On one occasion, God even said to Abraham, "Whatever Sarah tells you, listen to her" (Gen. 21:12). On an earlier occasion, however, Abraham listened to Sarah when he should not have done so and took Hagar as a second wife (Gen. 16:1-3).

The obstacles to faith that Sarah overcame differed from those that a man might encounter. First, she dealt with a husband whose fears resulted in her being placed into a harem on two separate occasions (Gen. 12:11-20; 20:1-18). Second, there was the problem of her barrenness. In an era in which inability to bear children often led to disgrace and rejection, she endured barrenness until she was *ninety years old,* at which point she bore *and raised* her miracle son, Isaac.

And finally, Sarah was forced to deal with her own bad advice: Before the birth of Isaac, Sarah had encouraged Abraham to take Hagar, her maid (a younger Egyptian woman), as a second wife so that Abraham could produce an heir. When Hagar bore Ishmael, they both managed to make life miserable for Sarah and she was forced to deal with the repercussions of her own bad advice.

A whole chapter (Genesis 23) is devoted to the death and burial of Sarah. Abraham mourned and wept for her. He purchased the first piece of property in the Promised Land as a burial site for Sarah. Isaac, too, mourned this remarkable woman. Only when he himself had married was he comforted concerning his mother's death.

Sarah encourages me. She honored her husband and treated him with deep respect. She overcame obstacles and became an example of those women in the Bible who "hoped in God" (1 Pet. 3:5-6). She made the list of heroes of the faith in Hebrews chapter 11—and she wasn't even perfect!

No list of great role models in the Bible would be complete without **Daniel**. In his youth Daniel was taken captive as a prisoner of war and transported to Babylon. He was brought into the palace, given a secular Babylonian education, and taught the language of the Chaldeans. His captors even changed his name, no doubt to impress on him his new status and to help him forget his former religion and country. His Hebrew name was Daniel (meaning "God is my judge"). His new name, Belteshazzar, must have been profoundly distressing to him: It honored Bel (or Baal), the chief god of the Chaldeans. Sad to contemplate, it is also likely that Daniel was castrated.[1]

Daniel, nevertheless, "made up his mind" not to compromise. He remained true to the God of Israel. At the same time, he must have studied hard to learn the Chaldean language and literature well, because when he stood before King Nebuchadnezzar, the king found him to be ten times superior to all his other wise men in every matter of wisdom and understanding about which he was consulted. Daniel reminds us of the proverb: "Do you see a man skilled in his work? He will stand before kings; he will not stand before obscure men" (Prov. 22:29). Daniel in fact stood before several kings! He lasted through the reigns of King Nebuchadnezzar, his descendant Belshazzar, Darius the Mede, and even into the first year of the reign of Cyrus, King of Persia.

When crises occurred, we never see Daniel in a panic, although his life was in danger on more than one occasion. His wisdom and his superior intellect may have been impressive, but his business ethics were even more so. As Daniel began to rise in favor and in power, others in the kingdom became jealous of him. They attempted to find grounds to accuse his business ethics but could find no evidence since "he was faithful, and no negligence or corruption was to be found in him" (Dan. 6:4). They watched him and eventually were able to bring an accusation against him only because he knelt before an open window three times a day and prayed to his God—a practice that had become illegal.

When Daniel learned that it was against the king's new law to pray to the true God, the God of Israel,, he could simply have prayed secretly behind closed doors. Compromise is so easy to rationalize! What if he had stopped praying publicly and justified it so that he could still keep his job? He could have argued that by praying secretly he would still be able to "make a difference" for God. But compromise would have given the impression that Daniel no longer prayed to the God of Israel. For this reason, Daniel risked his life (spending the night with some hungry lions) to remain faithful to God.

Daniel lived well into old age and maintained his sterling character to the end. A man of prayer, he persevered and fasted to get answers from God. Daniel overcame enormous obstacles. He lived through terrible experiences in his youth that we can hardly imagine. His example reminds us not to allow the past to control our lives. He encourages us to be steadfast to the end, to be people of believing prayer, and to maintain an exemplary testimony in a secular culture.

For Further Thought . . .

1. Although Sarah is held up as a role model, twice she went along with Abraham when he concealed the fact that she was his wife (Gen. 12:10-20 and 20:1-18). Was she right to do this? What about 1 Peter 3:6, which states that "you have become her children *if you do what is right* without being frightened by any fear"?

2. Do your own study of Elizabeth (Luke 1) as a positive role model in later life. What kind of obstacles did she overcome?

3. Consider the conduct of Joseph and Daniel as they functioned in a secular society. What obstacles do Christians face in the workplace today as they try to live consistently to honor God—especially late in their careers?

4. What has been the greatest obstacle in your own life to following the Lord and serving Him faithfully and effectively? In time, were you able to overcome this?

5. Obstacles from our past can also serve as excuses for failure to grow spiritually. Have you observed this? Have you experienced it? Comment.

Praying Always:
Samuel and Anna

*The effective prayer of a righteous man
can accomplish much.*

—JAMES 5:16

"The LORD changed His mind" (Ex. 32:14). Or, as it is put in the King James Version, "The LORD repented" concerning what He had announced He would do (Amos 7:3, 6; Jer. 26:19). It is electrifying to find such statements made in response to prayer. Does prayer really change things? Godly men and women in the pages of Scripture believed that it was so.

When it comes to prayer, as E. M. Bounds has written, "No half-hearted, half-brained, half-spirited effort will do for this serious, all-important, heavenly business. The whole heart, the whole brain, and the whole spirit must be engaged in the matter of praying, which is to affect so mightily the characters and destinies of men."[1]

One cannot think of great role models in the Bible without noticing the prominence of prayer in their lives. Abraham, Moses, Hannah, David, Hezekiah, Daniel, and the apostle Paul (to name only a sample) come readily to mind.

Like Daniel, whom we considered in the previous chapter, the prophet **Samuel** was also known as a man of integrity and a man of prayer. Born during the period of the judges to a godly woman named Hannah, Samuel was dedicated to God even before his birth. When Samuel was very young, his parents brought him to the tabernacle at Shiloh to be raised by Eli, the leading priest. Early in life, Samuel came to know the Lord. He grew spiritually and soon was serving faithfully both as a judge of Israel and as a prophet of the Lord.

In old age Samuel called on the people of Israel to affirm his integrity, saying,

"Whose ox have I taken, or whose donkey have I taken, or whom have I defrauded? Whom have I oppressed, or from whose hand have I taken a bribe to blind my eyes with it? I will restore it to you" (1 Sam. 12:2-5).

There were no accusations. The people agreed: Nothing marred Samuel's record. Unfortunately, the same could not be said for Samuel's sons. Samuel had hoped that his sons would replace him as judges of Israel. However, they did not follow in their father's footsteps. They took bribes, perverted justice, and were motivated by the love of money (1 Sam. 8:1-5). How that must have broken Samuel's heart. The vacuum of prospective leadership led Israel to demand a king. Samuel prayed to the Lord, and although their demand for a king displeased God and was a rejection of His direct leadership over the nation, God instructed Samuel to anoint Saul as king.

Samuel loved the people of Israel and served them with a tender heart. He encouraged them and reminded them that God would keep His promises and never abandon His people. When Saul showed himself unfit to rule, Samuel rebuked him and denounced him, but he also cared about Saul. He grieved so long over Saul's downfall that God told him it was time to move on and to anoint David as the next king (1 Sam. 16:1).

Above all, Samuel was a mighty intercessor. Time and time again, when the people of Israel strayed, Samuel interceded. On one occasion he said, "Far be it from me that I should sin against the LORD by ceasing to pray for you; but I will instruct you in the good and right way" (1 Sam. 12:23).

Even though Samuel's sons turned out badly, he must have prayed often for his grandchildren. His grandson Heman rose to fame in Israel as one of three chief musicians in charge of music for the tabernacle. Heman had a special place close to David's heart and is referred to as "the king's seer." Fourteen of Samuel's great-grandsons and three of his great-granddaughters ministered under Heman's direction, singing and playing musical instruments to the glory of God (1 Chron. 6:31-33; 25:1-7).

Are you saddened by the trends of society? Are you disappointed in the current leaders of the government, as Samuel was of Saul? Do you have a wayward son or daughter who has broken your heart? Remember Samuel, another memorable role-model, who never gave up and who considered it a sin to stop praying for his people.

In **Anna the Prophetess** we have an example of a godly woman of prayer who served God for most of her life, remaining faithful even in old age. After only seven years of marriage, her husband died. She then lived as a widow to the age of eighty-four. The Bible tells us that she did not leave the temple area but served God with fastings and prayers night and day (Luke 2:36-38).

She lived to see the baby Jesus brought to the temple for the first time. Instantly she recognized that He was the One who would bring redemption to His people. Not content to keep that information to herself, she spoke of Him to all those in Jerusalem who were looking for the promise of the Messiah.

Are you a little hesitant to speak to others about your faith? Have you drawn into a shell and stopped serving the Lord because you are a widow and no longer have your husband to lean on? Do you think you are too old to serve and to make a difference at your church? Think about Anna the next time you are tempted to say, "Oh, let the younger ones do it; I've served my time."

For Further Thought . . .

1. In a message to Ezekiel, God twice refers to three men who were role models of prayer. All three lived well into old age. Who were they, and what does God say about them? (Ezek. 14:14, 20).

2. Simeon apparently prayed for many years before the desire of his heart was granted. What did he live to see before his death? (Luke 2:25-35).

3. Identify the biggest obstacle to *consistent* prayer in your own life. What could you do to overcome it? *Will* you take steps to deal with it?

4. What is the longest period of time you prayed for something before God answered your prayers? What are you still praying about that has not yet been answered?

5. What conclusions about Moses and Samuel can we draw from what God said about them to the prophet Jeremiah (Jer. 15:1)?

6. Prayers are not always answered as we desire! Study the following verses and write down what you learn about *un*answered prayer: James 4:3; 2 Corinthians 12:7-9; 2 Samuel 12:15-20; 1 Peter 3:7; Micah 3:4.

Snared by Worldliness:
Noah and Demas

You adulteresses, do you not know that friendship
with the world is hostility toward God? Therefore
whoever wishes to be a friend of the world makes
himself an enemy of God.

—JAMES 4:4

If we were inclined to doubt the importance of studying the Old Testament, the writers of the New Testament are quick to remind us that, "Whatever was written in earlier times was written for our instruction, so that through perseverance and the encouragement of the Scriptures we might have hope" (Rom. 15:4). The apostle Paul wrote to the Corinthians that the things which happened to the people of Israel in former days "happened as examples for us" so that we would avoid their pitfalls and the consequences that followed (1 Cor. 10:6-11).

Many times we learn our most valuable

lessons in life from the bad examples that have touched our lives. In *A Foxfire Christmas*, Carolyn Stradley writes about a scarring experience in her youth that taught her to be lavishly hospitable. She was alone, hungry, and turned away without food from a minister's house on Christmas Day. Today she has two refrigerators, and just in case someone should drop in she cooks enough for a football team on Christmas Day![1] My mother-in-law, Ruth, used to entertain me with stories of her terrible mother-in-law. Ruth was easy to love; she learned how *not* to be a mother-in-law by observing hers!

In the Bible there is no shortage of bad examples. There are excellent reasons why people today do not ordinarily name their children Ahab or Jezebel, Judas or Herod. Herod the Great, for example, was ruling in Jerusalem when he ordered the execution of all babies under the age of two that had been born in Bethlehem. Among others whom Herod murdered were his wife and his own sons. In a play on Greek words, Caesar Augustus, hearing of these atrocities, joked that it was safer to be Herod's pig (*hus*) than his son (*huios*)!

Herod certainly knew that he was hated, because shortly before his death, he gave orders for the nobles of Judea be rounded up and held at the local hippodrome. He wanted them all to be murdered at the exact time of his death so that there would be plenty of mourning and lamentation at his funeral![2] (He apparently had an accurate idea of the esteem in which he was held by his subjects.) Herod's order was countermanded before his death.

We could add others to the list of egregiously bad examples, such as Delilah, wicked Queen Athaliah, and Jehoram, the fifth king of Judah, who died "with no one's regret," as it says in 2 Chronicles 21:20. Such cases, however, do not represent people whom we take seriously as God-fearing believers. We do not identify with them or compare our lives with theirs.

More cautionary examples for us are those with whom we might identify—people who seem to be followers of the true God of the Bible but who nevertheless disappoint us in later life. At what point do they make wrong choices? What causes their downward slide?

The story of "Noah and the ark" is so familiar to us as a children's story that it is hard to step out from the superficiality of the picture books and meet the real man. In an age of wickedness and violence, **Noah** found favor in the eyes of the Lord. He is called both a righteous man and one who was blameless in his time. Of even more significance, the Bible says that "Noah walked with God," a phrase used of only two men in the Bible—Enoch and Noah. John Wesley, commenting on this expression, wrote:

> He walked with God . . . in his generation, even in that corrupt degenerate age. It is easy to be religious when

73

religion is in fashion; but it is an evidence of strong faith to swim against the stream, and to appear for God, when no one else appears for him: so Noah did, and it is upon record to his immortal honour.[3]

God told Noah that He would destroy all flesh and establish His covenant with Noah and his family. He gave Noah specific directions on how to build an enormous barge-like structure to preserve animal life. Noah obeyed, responding to God's warning "by faith," and thus became one of those listed on God's honor roll of the faithful (Heb. 11:7). He demonstrates for us that real faith produces action and obedience. The Bible also calls Noah "a preacher of righteousness" (2 Peter 2:5). He must have continued to warn people of the coming judgment, but sadly saw no converts—not an easy life for a preacher.

Eventually, as God had promised, the flood inundated the earth and all except those in the ark perished. Noah and his family survived to walk again on a drying planet. Noah then took up farming and planted a vineyard.

From the closing years of his life we learn of only one incident: Noah became drunk. In connection with this episode, he lay naked in his tent and was, apparently, treated disrespectfully by his son Ham. Are we justified in being critical of Noah's drunkenness in this case?

Commentators are inclined to be charitable toward Noah on the assumption that even though fermentation must have occurred before the flood, this may have been Noah's first exposure to the effects of fermented grapes. It is still a sad note on which to leave this hero of the faith. Noah's example should have served as a warning to future generations against excessive drinking. Unhappily, the later history of the Bible documents numerous other cases of drunkenness that led to differing kinds of sordid conduct—to lewdness, nakedness, and even murder and incest.[4]

If you grew up in a home where drunkenness occurred frequently (as I did), you would wish that many more people took the lesson of Noah to heart. According to the American Academy of Family Physicians, "One-third of older alcoholic persons develop a problem with alcohol in later life."[5] Could the immoderate use of alcohol pose a problem even for *Christians* as they age? It would seem so. Some of the many admonitions against excessive drinking in the Bible are addressed specifically to *older* men and *older* women: It is "older men" who are instructed to be temperate [sober, KJV], and "older women" who are warned not to be enslaved to much wine (Titus 2:2-3).[6]

Not all the accounts of those who slipped in later life are told at great length. The story of **Demas**, who did not end well (as far as we know), is perhaps the briefest in all of Scripture. The Bible does not tell us when Demas professed faith in the Lord Jesus and began to travel with the apostle Paul. The first mention of Demas appears in Paul's letter to the Colossians, written in AD 60 or 61. At the time, Paul was in his first imprisonment, from which he was later released, and he was given limited freedom. Visitors came and went, and one of them was Demas.

As Paul closed his letter to the church at Colossae, he included greetings from those who were with him. After naming believers who were fellow Jews ("from the circumcision"), he next mentioned those who were Gentiles, including Luke, the beloved physician, and Demas. Both men sent greetings to the Christians living in Colossae (Col. 4:14), suggesting that they were already known to them.

The next mention of Demas occurs in Paul's letter to Philemon written at about the same time. Once again, Paul closed his letter with words of greeting from those who were with him: "Epaphras, my fellow prisoner in Christ Jesus, greets you, as do Mark, Aristarchus, Demas, Luke, *my fellow workers*" (Philem. 1:23-24, italics added). Paul uses the Greek word συνεργοι = *sunergoi*, meaning one who works, toils, or labors together with another. Thus Demas was not just a casual visitor to the jail but one who was involved in Christian ministry and who enjoyed the privilege of working personally alongside Paul.

Several years of Paul's ministry passed before we find the next and last mention of Demas in the Bible.

Paul had been released from his previous imprisonment referred to in Colossians and Philemon. He then had continued to travel and serve the Lord until he was re-arrested. He was now in his second and last imprisonment, and he knew he was soon to be executed (2 Tim. 4:6-8). His closing remarks to Timothy contain this sad statement: "Make every effort to come to me soon; for Demas, having loved this present world, has deserted me and gone to Thessalonica" (2 Tim. 4:9-10).

Some commentators have attempted to put a positive spin on the above statement, but the language Paul used is clear. Demas was not off on some missionary journey; he had *deserted* Paul. The Greek word translated "deserted" is strong and negative, used again by Paul in verse 16: "At my first defense no one supported me, but all *deserted* me; may it not be counted against them" (italics added).

The phrase Paul used, "having loved this present world" (2 Tim. 4:10), is also fraught with meaning. It is rare in the New Testament to see the Greek word for "love" that appears here (αγαπαω = *agapao*; noun *agape*) used in this fashion. In the minds of many people, *agape* love is associated only with *God's* love. It is the unselfish, God-like love husbands are to have for their wives and we all are to have for our enemies (Eph. 5:25; Matt. 5:44). How can one "love the world" with this type of love?

The meaning of *agape* love cannot be restricted to God's love. It would be more accurate to define *agape* as a love seated in the will and rooted in deliberate choice rather than feelings. The decision Demas made was the willful, deliberate choice to set his affection on the world. He counted the cost and found that he preferred the world to the hardships that Christians might be called on to face in this life.

Although such usage of *agape* is uncommon, a similar example occurs in John 3:19: "This is the judgment, that the Light has come into the world, and men loved [αγαπαω = *agapao*] the darkness rather than the Light, for their deeds were evil." Unbelievers make a deliberate choice: darkness.

The Bible warns believers:

> "Do not love the world nor the things in the world. If anyone loves the world, the love of the Father is not in him. For all that is in the world, the lust of the flesh and the lust of the eyes and the boastful pride of life, is not from the Father, but is from the world" (1 John 2:15-16).

On the evening before His crucifixion, Jesus said to His disciples:

> "If the world hates you, you know that it has hated Me before it hated you. If you were of the world, the world would love its own; but because you are not of the world, but I chose you out of the world, because of this the world hates you" (John 15:18-19).

The lesson from the life of Demas is deceptively simple: Watch out for worldliness. Warnings in the New Testament abound; the hard part is application. No professing Christian likes to think of him or herself as "worldly." It is easy to make up a set of rules to define worldliness. Is it playing cards? Wearing make-up or jewelry? Going to the movies? Buying expensive cars? What about wasting time at the computer? Owning a television? Devoting more time to sports than to serving God? Inevitably such a list excludes our own choices!

Are you worldly? We do not escape choices leading to worldliness in old age. Lists of rules have never been very effective in stamping out worldliness. It is not *law* but *grace* that teaches us not to sin: "For the *grace* of God has appeared . . . instructing us to deny ungodliness and worldly desires and to live sensibly, righteously and godly in the present age" (Titus 2:11-12, italics added). In the long run, we will not love the world less until we learn to love God more.

For Further Thought . . .

1. How would you define *worldliness*? What is meant by the word *world* as it is used in 1 John 2:15-16 and John 15:18-19?

2. How have your convictions concerning worldliness changed over time?

3. Jesus sent His followers "into the world" (John 17:18). How can we be effective reaching people *in* the world and still not be "*of* the world" (John 15:19; 17:14)?

4. Amazingly, Lot is called a *righteous* man in 2 Peter 2:7. Examine the worldly choices he made that led to degradation and a ruined life. See Genesis chapters 13, 14, and 19.

5. What might be some of the reasons for increased alcoholic consumption among the elderly?

6. What are your own convictions about alcoholic consumption? Why do you hold the views that you do?

Snared by Sex:
David and Solomon

Do not be deceived, God is not mocked; for whatever a man sows, this he will also reap.

—GALATIANS 6:7

It is not often that we think of **King David** in the category of "not-so-good" role models. David, after all, is the one uniquely described in the Bible as "a man after God's own heart" (1 Sam. 13:14; Acts 13:22). From humble beginnings he rose to become the second king of Israel. He was a man with a heart for worship who deeply loved and appreciated God.

By the time David was about forty years old, he had married several wives who had borne him several sons. He was residing in a palace in Jerusalem, and, as 2 Samuel chapter 11 opens, it was spring time, the time when kings go out to battle. On this occasion David sent his troops to battle with Joab in command, but David himself stayed home.

Perhaps he was getting a little tired, a little lazy, or maybe he was having what we would call a mid-life crisis.

Whatever the reason, when evening came, David was walking around on the roof of his house when he looked down and saw a woman bathing. She was beautiful, and he sent a servant to inquire about her identity. David learned that her name was Bathsheba and that she was married to Uriah the Hittite, who served in David's army. At this all-important crossroads in his life, David made a wrong turn. He had Bathsheba brought to him and committed adultery.

David no doubt expected to get away with his sin. After all, he was the king. Who would know? Christians today who know their Bibles know better. "The eyes of the LORD are in every place, watching the evil and the good" (Prov. 15:3).The book of Hebrews adds these cautionary words: "If you are without discipline, of which all have become partakers, then you are illegitimate children and not sons" (Heb. 12:8). Are you a real child of God? Then be sure you will experience discipline. The process of discipline for David began when Bathesheba learned that she was pregnant and sent word to David.

The problem with doing one wrong thing is that it quickly compounds. In the absence of immediate repentance, lying or other forms of treachery sprout like weeds to cover up the first offense. In this case, David sent for Bathsheba's husband Uriah to come home and report on the war. If Uriah slept with his wife while on leave, the child born to Bathsheba would appear to be Uriah's child. Unfortunately for David's plan, noble Uriah felt it was wrong to enjoy the pleasures of home life while his comrades were continuing to fight a war. He left without visiting his wife.

David then made another seriously wrong decision. He instructed his general to position Uriah at the front of the battle and have the troops pull back from him. Thus Uriah conveniently died in battle, Bathsheba mourned, and when her mourning period was over, she married David and bore him a son. Where was God in all this? The chapter ends with these ominous words: "But the thing that David had done was evil in the sight of the Lord."

After David committed adultery, months went by without repentance. (Did he sense a coldness in his heart toward God? Did he find it difficult to pray?) In time, God sent Nathan the prophet to David with a story to tell. It featured a selfish rich man who stole a beloved lamb from a poor man who had only one little lamb that he had brought up and nourished. When David heard the story, his anger blazed. He said to Nathan, "The man who has done this deserves to die. He must make restitution for the lamb fourfold, because he . . . had no compassion" (2 Sam. 12:5-6).

In a flash the truth was out: "You are the man!" said Nathan the prophet. David showed deep remorse and acknowledged his sin against the Lord. God forgave David and spared his life (which, under the Law of Moses, would have been forfeited because of adultery). But forgiveness did not wipe out the consequences. Trouble soon descended on his household. For the "lamb" (Bathsheba) he had taken, David did indeed restore fourfold: Over the course of the remaining twenty to thirty years of his life he lost four of his sons—one born to Bathsheba, then Amnon, Absalom, and Adonijah.

Today sexual sin is rampant and touches the lives of believers as well as unbelievers. What lessons can we learn from these events in the life of David? How could this special, godly man fall into such devastating sin? The Bible teaches that any time we think we are immune to sin we are on dangerous ground. Incidents from Old Testament times "happened to them as an example, and they were written for our instruction. . . . Therefore *let him who thinks he stands take heed that he does not fall*" (1 Cor. 10:11-12, italics added).

It is helpful to consider and learn from the facts of David's case:

1) These events happened in the last half of David's life. We do not become immune to sexual or other sins because we have walked with the Lord for many years or because we have attained a good reputation, recognition, or privilege. Many older men and women succumb to adultery and abandon their spouses. Even in Puritan times there were those like the Reverend Stephen Bachiler of New Hampshire who was excommunicated on a charge of sexual immorality at age seventy-eight![1] Continual watchfulness is the answer. "Watch over your heart with all diligence" (Prov. 4:23).

2) David's repentance did not eliminate consequences. Always keeping the consequences of sin firmly in mind is a great deterrent. We have the naive idea in our society that saying "I'm sorry," or "I repent," ends all consequences. Forgiveness restores our relationship with God (the most important thing), but does not wipe out all consequences. A spouse may pursue divorce. Children may become disillusioned and bitter and refuse to attend church ever again.

In the case of a church leader, adultery results in disqualification for office even after repentance. Such a leader no longer has a "good reputation" and is no longer "above reproach"—two qualifications stipulated for those exercising spiritual leadership (1 Tim. 3:2, 7; Titus 1:5-7). Proverbs 6:33 makes it clear that, in the case of sexual sin, "His reproach will not be blotted out."

3) David's repentance was genuine, heart-felt, and thorough. Psalm 51, written by David after these events, helps us better understand the greatness of this man. David made no attempt to justify himself.

By writing a song (Psalm 51) about what he had done, he made his repentance public. He did not gloss over it. He did not label it a "mistake," but used terms like *transgression, sin, iniquity,* and *bloodguiltiness.*

4) God's promises to David remained intact in spite of his sin. There is hope after sin and repentance. God continued to love and esteem David. He remained the standard of greatness for future kings. David feared God and his heart wholly belonged to God. In Psalm 103, he celebrated God's lovingkindness and forgiveness when he wrote:

"He has not dealt with us according to our sins,
Nor rewarded us according to our iniquities.
For as high as the heavens are above the earth,
So great is His lovingkindness
toward those who fear Him.
As far as the east is from the west,
So far has He removed our transgressions from us"
(103:10-12).

David understood that his sin was no longer a barrier between him and God.

Solomon, the son of David and Bathsheba, was conceived and born some time after David and Bathsheba's first son had died. The name Solomon, meaning *peaceful,* is related to the Hebrew word for peace (*shalom*), and his reign indeed marked a unique time of peace and prosperity for the nation of Israel. Unfortunately, Solomon provides us with another example of a man who began admirably but slipped badly in later years.

Before his death, David counseled Solomon with these weighty words:

> "As for you, my son Solomon, know the God of your father, and serve Him with a whole heart and a willing mind; for the LORD searches all hearts, and understands every intent of the thoughts. If you seek Him, He will let you find Him; but if you forsake Him, He will reject you forever" (1 Chron. 28:9).

Very early in Solomon's reign, he prayed: "O LORD my God, You have made Your servant king in place of my father David, yet I am but a little child; I do not know how to go out or come in" (1 Kings 3:7). He expressed his sense of inadequacy and asked only that God would give him an understanding heart to be able to rule and judge God's people with wisdom.

The modesty of Solomon's request pleased the Lord, and He granted his desire. He promised to make Solomon uniquely wise so that no one before him or after him would be as wise. In addition, God promised to give him two things he had not asked for: riches and honor. Soon Solomon was demonstrating his God-given wisdom in numerous and interesting ways: He rendered just verdicts in court; he loved science and used his expertise breeding cattle and horses; he raised crops; he set up extensive trade with foreign countries; he spoke 3,000 proverbs; and he wrote 1,005 songs (1 Kings 4:32).

When Solomon finished building the temple for God in Jerusalem, he assembled all the leaders of the nation for its dedication. Solomon then blessed the people, reminded them of God's promises, and prayed. His public prayer, one of the longest prayers in the Bible, is full of theological awareness and shows Solomon's keen insight into God's mind and heart (1 Kings 8:22-53).

1) He understood God's omniscience.

"You alone know the hearts of all the sons of men" (v. 39).

2) He understood God's omnipresence.

"Heaven and the highest heaven cannot contain You, how much less this house which I have built!" (v. 27).

3) He understood God's faithfulness.

"Not one word has failed of all His good promise" (v. 56).

4) He understood God's omnipotence.

God could defeat their enemies, send rain, forgive sin, and answer prayer (v. 33-37).

Soon, however, Solomon's attention shifted to things other than worship. He developed a taste for luxury worthy of an oriental sultan. David's palace was not good enough; Solomon built a new one for himself. It took him seven years to build God's temple and thirteen years to build his own palace. He then built a separate palace for his queen, the daughter of the Pharaoh of Egypt. In time, other dwellings were built.

During this time of prosperity, Solomon apparently was not having his "daily devotions"! If he had been, he would have been reminded of laws in the Bible which were binding for all kings (Deut. 17:14-20): (1) The king was to daily read (and make his own copy of) the Law of Moses; (2) He was *not* to multiply horses for himself (but Solomon did); (3) He was *not* to greatly increase gold and silver for himself (but Solomon did); and (4) He was *not* to multiply wives for himself (and Solomon *surely* did).[2] Solomon had, in fact, seven hundred wives and three hundred concubines!

Even though the Israelites were commanded not to marry or associate with people from certain nations, such as the Hittites, Solomon loved and married women from those forbidden nations (Deut. 7:2-3). We then read this sad verse: *"For when Solomon was old*, his wives turned his heart away after other gods; and his heart was not wholly devoted to the LORD his God, as the heart of David his father had been" (1 Kings 11:4, italics added). Solomon actually built

89

shrines for various idols, burned incense in those places, and sacrificed to idols.

What could possibly account for such a shift in Solomon's behavior? I like to imagine what some of the dialog might have been between Solomon and his foreign wives. Perhaps on some occasion one of his wives said this:

> "I don't see why I can't have my own place to worship like you do. You needn't be so narrow-minded. It's not as if I'm asking you to stop worshiping Jehovah, but I miss the fun festivals we celebrate honoring Ashtoreth. They're harmless, and you'd love them! There's lots of lively music and dancing. They're not boring and straight-laced like your worship at the temple."

Perhaps he simply got tired of saying "no." How many people (especially in their later years, when they are weary) are worn down by the persistent nagging or pleadings of a spouse and finally give in— agreeing to something they know to be wrong? Solomon's downward slide was not caused primarily by lust (as in David's case), but by compromise with apostasy—the inability to say "no," and to understand the importance of separation. Verses in the New Testament remind us:

> "Do not be bound together with unbelievers; for what partnership have righteousness and lawlessness, or what fellowship has light with darkness? Or what

harmony has Christ with Belial, or what has a believer in common with an unbeliever? Or what agreement has the temple of God with idols? . . . 'Therefore, come out from their midst and be separate,' says the Lord" (2 Cor. 6:14-17).

There is no room for compromise with idolatry and apostasy. And when it comes to marriage, widows are also cautioned that while they are free to remarry after the death of a husband, they are only to marry "in the Lord" (1 Cor. 7:39).

No doubt a contributing factor in Solomon's move away from God was also his love of luxury. While it is not wrong to be wealthy, it can be a serious source of temptation. "It is hard for a rich man to enter the kingdom of heaven," Jesus said, after the Rich Young Ruler walked away from an invitation to become a follower of Jesus (Matt. 19:23). In the Parable of the Sower and the Seed, Jesus taught about those who allow the Word of God to become choked out by "worries and riches and pleasures of this life." They are the ones who bring no fruit to maturity (Luke 8:14).

Surely in Solomon's case, his love of luxury bore evil fruit. Perhaps he was thinking of himself in old age when he wrote, "A poor yet wise lad is better than an old and foolish king who no longer knows how to receive instruction" (Eccl. 4:13).

For Further Thought . . .

1. What factors in David's life may have played a role in his susceptibility to adultery?

2. Study chapters 5, 6, and 7 of Proverbs. List the consequences of adultery that are described in those chapters.

3. AIDS cases among people age fifty and older in the United States have jumped 22 percent since 1991.[3] What changes in society may have contributed to increased promiscuity and skyrocketing cases of sexually transmitted diseases (STDs) among the elderly?

4. What is the difference between sexual temptation and sin? When does temptation cross the line and become sin? (Matt. 5:28; James 1:13-15).

5. How are the sexual temptations of older widows and widowers to be handled without violating principles of Scripture? See 1 Thessalonians 4:3-7 for help with this.

Pride Goes Before a Fall:
Miriam and Uzziah

When pride comes, then comes dishonor.

—PROVERBS 11:2

When you grow up in a family with two famous brothers it's easy to be overlooked, even if you are the oldest. Moses and Aaron were the famous brothers, and **Miriam** was their older sister. Miriam no doubt had responsibilities early in life keeping an eye on her infant brother Moses and keeping him quiet so that the Egyptians would not find him and kill him. When Moses was three months old and it was no longer possible to hide him effectively, it was Miriam who accompanied the little basket containing her baby brother to the Nile River and watched to observe his rescue.

Many years passed, during which Moses was reared in the palace of Pharaoh. The time came when Moses saw an Egyptian beating a Hebrew slave. He intervened, killing the Egyptian, and was forced to flee for his life. Perhaps Moses was able to maintain some contact with his family during his forty-year period of exile. The Bible does not say. Meanwhile, Aaron and Miriam continued their existence as slaves under the heavy yoke of the Egyptians.

The next time we encounter Miriam is at the crossing of the Red Sea (Exodus 15). What a time of glorious celebration that must have been! The Israelites had just observed an astounding miracle where the waters parted, allowing them to cross, and then returned, drowning the Egyptian army. Their time of bondage in Egypt was over! A song of celebration followed, sung by Moses and the sons of Israel. Miriam led the women in the responsive chorus, and they followed her lead with timbrels and dancing.

By this time, Miriam was known to the people of Israel as the sister of Moses and of Aaron, which would have elevated her status in the community. She was exercising some degree of leadership among the women of Israel. In addition, she is referred to here as a "prophetess" (one who speaks for God). God chose not only Moses and Aaron, but also Miriam for special roles during this time in Israel's history. The Lord later reminded His people, "I brought you up from the land of Egypt and ransomed you from the house of slavery, and I sent before you Moses, Aaron *and Miriam*" (Micah 6:4, italics added). No wonder Matthew Henry speaks of both Aaron and Miriam as "joint commissioners with Moses for the deliverance of Israel."[1]

How easily pride follows prestige! Sadly, the next time we encounter Miriam, she and Aaron are leading a rebellion against Moses. Miriam, whose name appears first in this incident (Num. 12:1), seems to be the instigator, and Aaron, who had an unfortunate history of going-along-with-the-crowd (Ex. 32:1-25), joins with her.

They spoke against Moses because of his marriage to a Cushite (Ethiopian) woman. Whether the woman referred to here was Zipporah (the first wife of Moses) or a second woman whom he married after her death is irrelevant to the story. Perhaps Miriam resented this woman for infringing on her sphere of influence, or perhaps both Miriam and Aaron objected to her out of racial prejudice.

God moved swiftly to affirm that Moses was, indeed, His choice to be in charge. He summoned Moses and Aaron and Miriam to come to the tent of meeting. There God made it clear that Moses stood in a unique relationship with Him. God's anger burned against Miriam and Aaron, and when the cloud of God's glory had withdrawn, Miriam was leprous, as white as snow.

Aaron was quick to humbly apologize for his part in the rebellion and to intercede for Miriam. Moses, too, begged God to heal his sister. It is interesting that

God refused to heal her immediately. (Did she need to be humbled? Would the lesson have been lost if God had healed her instantly?) And so for seven days, Miriam was shut up in isolation outside the camp until God healed her.

What do you think caused the downward slide of Miriam in old age? (She would have been at least in her eighties when this act of rebellion transpired.) How easily we become puffed up after tasting a little power, prestige, or authority. It is difficult to step back to a subordinate role when we have tasted leadership and success. We live in a rebellious society where any call for submission and humble service is usually greeted with resentment, whether within the family, in society at large, or in the church.

The Bible warns us about following arrogant, self-centered leaders, or those who love to have first place in the church (1 Tim. 3:6; 3 John 9). Perhaps you have stepped down from a position of power and influence. Are you making it difficult for those who have risen to take your place? From Miriam's example, it is obvious that women as well as men can become jealous and resentful of the authority of others, especially after they have tasted some recognition and authority of their own.

Miriam's story also cautions us about prejudice. Do we feel superior to or patronizing toward those of another culture? What attitudes do we display to those of foreign descent who travel in our country or settle here permanently as residents? The Israelites were sternly warned: "The stranger who resides with you shall be to you as the native among you, and you shall love him as yourself, for you were aliens in the land of Egypt; I am the LORD your God" (Lev. 19:34; Deut. 10:19).

Uzziah, also known as Azariah, was one of the few really good kings of Judah. He reigned for fifty-two years, longer than any other king of Judah, with the exception of Manasseh. He came to the throne at age sixteen and set his heart to seek God. Like Joash before him, Uzziah was fortunate to have a mentor (named Zechariah) who taught him the fear of the Lord. A man of diverse interests and abilities, Uzziah dug cisterns for water, raised livestock, and grew crops in the hills and in the Shephelah. The Bible states that "he loved the soil" (2 Chron. 26:10).

In war, he waged successful campaigns against the Philistines (long-standing enemies of the nation of Israel), against the Arabs, the Ammonites, and others. The army under Uzziah was an elite, well-equipped force of 307,500 men provided with shields, spears, helmets, body armor, bows, and sling stones. His architectural interests led him to build towers in the wilderness and towers at the gates of Jerusalem. He equipped the towers in Jerusalem with newly invented engines of war able to shoot arrows and gigantic stones. His fame, in fact, extended to the border of Egypt.

The Bible states that *as long as Uzziah sought the Lord*, God caused him to prosper. "He was marvelously helped until he was strong. But when he became strong, his heart was so proud that he acted corruptly" (2 Chron. 26:15-16). What is it about human nature? Why is it that people who reach the pinnacle of success often feel they can dispense with God's help and God's rules?

The form that pride took in Uzziah's case seems at first to be *spiritually* motivated. How could his actions possibly be wrong? He simply entered the temple of God intending to burn incense to the Lord on the altar of incense. The problem was that only priests from the tribe of Levi were permitted to enter the temple. Uzziah was from the tribe of Judah, and he was not a priest. When eighty priests confronted him to prevent his doing so, he became angry. God's discipline was immediate and stopped him in his tracks. As the priests stared in horror, leprosy broke out on his forehead. Uzziah was quickly removed from the premises and lived as a leper in a separate house to the day of his death.

When pride is present, it affects even the way we choose to worship. Worshiping *our* way when our way violates the clear directions of Scripture is perhaps the height of arrogance. In the time of Moses, God struck down two of Aaron's sons instantaneously because they disregarded God's holiness by offering incense unauthorized by God's laws (Lev. 10:1-3). King Saul was guilty of an offense similar to Uzziah's. He lost the crown for offering up burnt offerings and peace offerings to the Lord contrary to God's law and contrary to the instructions of the prophet Samuel (1 Sam. 13:9-14). In David's time, a Levite named Uzza helped transport the ark of God in an unauthorized way and died instantly because he disobeyed the Law.[2]

Could God make it any clearer? These examples should make us pause. All of these men were supposedly involved in "honoring" God and "worshiping" Him. That is why worship needs to be informed and governed by Scripture. "There is a way which seems right to a man, but its end is the way of death" (Prov. 14:12).

The New Testament reinforces the importance of obedience. Jesus taught that those who worship God "*must* worship in spirit and truth" (John 4:24, italics added). He taught that those who desire to enter the kingdom of God "*must* be born again" (John 3:7, italics added). Similarly, when you choose leaders who are approved by God to exercise leadership in a church, they "*must* be above reproach" (Titus 1:7, italics added) and meet the qualifications God has established. These are not suggestions, but clear directions. We violate them at our peril.

For Further Thought . . .

1. Worship services in many churches have changed drastically in the past thirty or forty years. How can we tell if the way we worship is pleasing to God?

2. Pride caused the downward slide of many rulers in the Bible in their later years. What consequences tend to follow pride? If you wanted to guard against pride in your own life, what steps could you take?

3. Make a list of ten verses on the subject of pride that are especially meaningful and helpful to you. Laminate the list and keep it where you will see it often. For a start, see Proverbs 16:5, 18, and 19.

4. King Hezekiah was one of the "good" kings of Judah. Pride, however, marred his record at one point late in life. Do a character analysis of him in his final years after studying 2 Chronicles 32:24-26 and 2 Kings 20:12-19.

5. What are some of the subtle evidences of pride that come out in our conversations with one another—even in Christian circles?

Rejecting Wise Counsel:
Joash and Amaziah

*Advice is like mushrooms. The wrong kind
can prove fatal.*

—Anonymous

Joash (also known as Jehoash) became the eighth king of Judah. He is popularly known as "the boy king" because he was crowned king at the age of seven.[1] When his father Ahaziah died, Ahaziah's mother, the notorious Queen Athaliah (daughter of Ahab and Jezebel), murdered all of his sons (her grandchildren and step-grandchildren) and seized the throne for herself. Only one infant son of Ahaziah was safely hidden from Athaliah's murderous intentions: baby Joash.

For six years Joash remained hidden under the protection and care of the godly high priest, Jehoiada. In time, Jehoiada was able to organize support to overthrow Queen Athaliah so that Joash, a legitimate heir of King David, could be crowned. The day came when armed guards brought Joash out of hiding, put a crown on his head, and anointed him king. Queen Athaliah was executed, and thus began the reign of the boy king.

Immediately after Joash was crowned, Jehoiada made a covenant between the Lord, the king, and the people in which the people renewed their allegiance to the Lord. The people then went to the house of Baal, tore it down, smashed the images associated with Baal worship, and executed the priest of Baal. They rejoiced that wicked Queen Athaliah was dead. Once again the city of Jerusalem was quiet, and soon worship under the Levites was re-established at the temple of the Lord.

Jehoiada, the godly priest, continued to have a strong influence during the formative years of Joash. In fact, Jehoiada was the one who selected his wives! (2 Chron. 24:3). Under Jehoiada's tutelage, Joash determined to repair the temple of the Lord which had been defiled and badly damaged during Queen Athaliah's reign. Although the repairs were long delayed by lack of funds, eventually the money was raised and the temple was restored.

Jehoiada reached a "ripe old age," as the Bible puts it, and died. Ripe indeed! He was 130 years old at his death, having lived longer than any person mentioned in the Bible since the time of Amram, the father of Moses, about seven hundred years earlier. Jehoiada was so highly esteemed by the nation that he was buried among the kings of Israel.

Joash was now, for the first time, without his mentor, and we read this statement about his reign: "Jehoash [Joash] did right in the sight of the LORD *all his days in which Jehoiada the priest instructed him*" (2 Kings 12:2, italics added). So what about the days *after* Jehoiada?

Sad to say, things soon fell apart. The officials of Judah came before King Joash, and he listened to their unwise counsel. They influenced him to abandon the temple and abandon the Lord. Soon the nation was involved in perverted and idolatrous worship. The Lord sent prophets to bring them to repentance, but they would not listen. Finally the Spirit of God came on Zechariah, the son of Jehoiada the priest, and he spoke to the people saying, "Why do you transgress the commandments of the LORD and do not prosper? Because you have forsaken the LORD, He has also forsaken you" (2 Chron. 24:20).

Not only was Zechariah's message rejected, but *at the command of the king*, they stoned Zechariah to death in the temple courtyard. Needless to say, Joash ended badly. Without God's blessing, the nation lost a war with the Syrians, and Joash was murdered by his own servants for killing Jehoiada's son. The people did not even bury Joash in the tombs of the kings, as they had Jehoiada.

How can we explain what happened to Joash in the last years of his life? Here was a man raised from infancy to love and follow the Lord who nevertheless departed from the faith after the death of his mentor. It raises an obvious question: On whom do you lean for spiritual strength? Who keeps your feet on the straight and narrow path? Can we lean too heavily on a strong mentor or spiritual leader and never mature to the point where we can stand alone? God provides gifted people "some as apostles, and some as prophets, and some as evangelists, and some as pastors and teachers" to equip believers for ministry with the goal of *full maturity,* not ongoing dependence (Eph. 4:11-16).

Many times, parents are shocked and saddened when one of their adult children walks away from the faith. Often such children have been living on second-hand faith. Although they have learned all the right religious jargon, all the shibboleths of the faith, they have never developed or deepened their own personal relationship with God. Away from spiritual influence, they are prone to accept harmful counsel and follow bad advice.

In later life, this kind of falling-away from the faith may take a different form: A husband or wife dies, and the spiritual life of the remaining spouse plummets. I have observed such cases myself. The strong spouse, now deceased, used to provide order and accountability and encouragement in the faith. Perhaps he or she helped to compensate for weaknesses in the character of the remaining spouse. Once that person is gone, glaring defects come to the surface.

It is worth thinking about: In what way does your spouse compensate for the chinks in your spiritual armor? Are you the spiritually strong member of the team, or the weaker one? No spouse or mentor should function as our "Jehoiada" indefinitely. We are responsible for our own ongoing relationship with the Lord.

After the murder of Joash, his son **Amaziah** was crowned the ninth king of Judah at the age of twenty-five. Like his father before him, he began well, doing what was "right in the eyes of the Lord." As soon as the kingdom was firmly under Amaziah's control, he executed the men who had assassinated his father. But unlike the custom of the day, he did *not* execute the children of those men as well. He apparently knew and honored the command from the law of Moses that fathers were not to be executed for the crimes of their sons, and sons were not to be executed for the crimes of their fathers (Deut. 24:16).

Amaziah next organized the military, mustering an army of 300,000 men who were able to handle spear and shield. Additionally he hired another 100,000 men from the kingdom of Israel as mercenaries. His plans for battle were modified when a man of God came to him with a message from the Lord. He told Amaziah to send the mercenaries back to Israel, that God was not with Israel, and that God had the power to help him or to bring him down.

This time, Amaziah listened and obeyed. In spite of the economic loss, he did as he was instructed. With courage, Amaziah then led his own troops into battle against the Edomites. He conquered them at Sela (today usually identified with Petra—a formidable fortress) and returned to Judah flushed with victory. Unfortunately, he also brought back the gods of the Edomites, set them up as his gods, and worshiped them!

Soon the Lord sent a prophet with a question to ask the king: "Why have you sought the gods of the people who have not delivered their own people from your hand?" (2 Chron. 25:15). A good question! If the idols had not been able to deliver the Edomites, what possible good could they do Amaziah? The king stopped the prophet in mid sentence with a warning that if he continued to speak he would be struck down. The prophet managed a parting shot as he left. He told Amaziah that God would destroy him because of his idolatry and because he did not listen to the counsel he had just received.

Next we read that Amaziah "took counsel" and decided to go to war against Jehoash king of Israel (not to be confused with a different Jehoash, the former king of Judah). Amaziah no doubt was feeling quite cocky after his win against the Edomites, but this proposed war had no real justification. It would have been an aggressive rather than a defensive war.

When the king of Israel heard of Amaziah's plan, he urged him to give up his intentions, saying, "You have indeed defeated Edom, and your heart has become proud. Enjoy your glory and stay at home; for why should you provoke trouble so that you, even you, would fall, and Judah with you?" (2 Kings 14:10). But Amaziah was determined. He went to war, lost, and incurred heavy losses for the kingdom of Judah. Although he lived fifteen years after that fateful battle, he became a singularly unpopular king. Eventually a conspiracy arose against him. Amaziah fled to Lachish, but his enemies followed him there and assassinated him.

At the beginning of Amaziah's reign, we read this comment concerning him: "He did right in the sight of the LORD, yet not with a whole heart" (2 Chron. 25:2). It is worth thinking about the part of his heart that was *not* wholly the Lord's. What hidden potential for trouble exists when part of the heart is withheld from God's sovereign control? In Amaziah's case, success in war bred a sense of pride and power. What was he thinking when he removed idols from Edom and brought them home? Did he think of them at first as merely valuable objects of art? Perhaps he thought he was above the law.

When pride rules the heart, an unwillingness to listen to godly advice soon follows. First, Amaziah rejected the warning of the prophet who confronted him about his idolatry. Second, he chose the wrong counselors, who advised him to declare war on Israel. Third, he ignored the warning of the king of Israel, who advised him not to declare war. One of the characteristics of a fool, according to the book of Proverbs, is that he does not listen to good counsel (Prov. 12:15; 13:10).

Are we more prone to stubborn pride in our later years? Are we less likely to listen to godly counsel? Early in life we are used to being taught by others, but in time *we* become the teachers, the experts, the authorities in our chosen fields. We can easily imagine ourselves to be infallible and resent those who promote change. With inflexibility comes resistance to the counsel of others. There is no easy cure for this—just constant vigilance.

Pride is so inherently damaging to our relationship with God that it would be well to memorize a few of the more than one hundred verses in the Bible that speak to it. Especially sobering are the words of James 4:6: "God is opposed to the proud, but gives grace to the humble."

For Further Thought . . .

1. What do we learn about the seriousness of pride from James 4:6 and 1 Peter 5:5? What does it mean to have God *opposed* to you?

2. Both Joash and Uzziah benefited from having a mentor. The apostle Paul, too, was probably a mentor to Demas. Was there a time when you were helped by a similar relationship? Have you served as a mentor to others? What are the advantages and potential pitfalls of such an association?

3. What advice would you give to young Christians seeking counsel? How could you help steer them away from the wrong kind of counselor?

4. Rehoboam, son of King Solomon, was at least forty-years-old when he became king. How did he select those who would be his counselors? (2 Chron. 10). What were the results of his decision? What can we learn from his actions?

5. Do you think older people are less likely to respond positively to counsel and advice than younger ones? What about *you*?

Dangers to Watch and Choices to Make

Taking It a Bit Too Easy

Next to the very young, I suppose the very old are the most selfish.

—William Makepeace Thackery

Many of us can identify with the following verse taken from an old, familiar hymn:

> O to grace how great a debtor
> daily I'm constrained to be!
> Let Thy goodness, like a fetter,
> bind *my wandering heart* to Thee.
> *Prone to wander, Lord, I feel it,*
> *prone to leave the God I love;*
> Here's my heart, O take and seal it;
> seal it for Thy courts above.[1] (italics added)

Wandering. We wish that it were not so. Although we wander in a variety of ways and can stray at any age, it is worth considering what pitfalls we are most vulnerable to as we age and why we are susceptible to them. Someone at the age of seventy or eighty may not be dealing with sexual temptations to the same degree as a twenty-year-old. On the other hand, experts tell us that people over sixty are more likely to suffer from depression than any other age group, including teenagers.

Changes in our lifestyle and in our physical bodies expose us to different types of stresses, which in turn lead to temptations for which we may be unprepared. What are some of these areas that can keep us from hearing "Well done, thou good and faithful servant" from the Lord when we ultimately stand before Him?

One such area might be: taking it a bit too easy.

In his article, "Let's Hear It For Decrepitude," Melvin Maddocks wrote that outsiders to the older generation typically "bombard us with [advice] like 'Keep active,' an exhortation almost as meaningless as 'Have a nice day.' Who would argue for being inactive?"[2] Actually, "taking it a bit too easy" as we age can take many forms. It is not just physical laziness that creeps up on us but also intellectual, social, and spiritual laziness. In fact, if we are lazy in one of these areas, we probably struggle in all of them!

PHYSICAL

Let's distinguish first of all between slowing down physically, which is normal as you age, and just plain laziness. It is realistic to expect your energy level to diminish in later years. Even if you exercise regularly, you still will not have the same measure of energy at age seventy that you had at twenty. Rest is not a sin. Take a nap if you need it. Sit down with a good book. An argument *against* laziness is not an argument *for* constant, frenzied activity. You may have been too busy to smell the flowers when you were raising a family and had a full-time job—enjoy smelling them now!

Laziness is another matter. The Bible contains dozens of verses that deal with laziness, although in all my years of listening to sermons, I do not recall hearing a single one on the subject. "Sluggards" (lazy people) and their habits are a common theme of the book of Proverbs. In chapter 6, sluggards are invited to learn how *not* to be sluggards by observing the behavior of ants. These small creatures have "no chief, officer or ruler" as they work—no one to observe or supervise them, yet they work anyway (Prov. 6:7-8). Do you use your time well when no chief, officer, or ruler is watching you?

While laziness can be a problem at any age, it may be a greater problem when we are older because of a lack of structure in our lives. It was easier to manage your time when you *had* to get up with the alarm clock and fix breakfast for the children before they left for school. You *had* to get up to go to work. You *had* to get up to walk the dogs. But now, perhaps, the kids are married, you have retired, and your sweet little dogs are singing (barking?) with the angels.

Structure and discipline are even harder to maintain when you live alone. You can stay in bed until noon. You can cook for yourself, or choose not to cook at all, nibbling on snacks out of the refrigerator instead of eating regular meals. By the way, one characteristic of the sluggard is that he is too lazy to cook his food! (Proverbs 12:27). Who is to know if you decide to snack and watch television all day? Only God is watching.

Health problems may be a legitimate reason for cutting back physically, but they can also be a convenient excuse to avoid doing the things we are not in a mood to do. We have all known people who use health issues to get out of responsibilities and commitments that they simply do not feel like doing. A fellow-believer, Mamie Watson, provided a wonderful role model of old age for me. In church one day I remember her saying to me, "If I waited until I felt well, I would never be here." How true! Mamie had a rare disorder that could easily have given her an excuse to miss church much of the time, but she was highly disciplined and motivated to be there. I have seen young women like "Ellen" miss Bible study class because it rained! Yet I have also seen others, like an older woman with a broken ankle named Mildred, who *crawled* up a long flight of stairs and had someone carry her walker to the top, just so she could attend Bible study.

One reason it is hard to fight against laziness is that our society condones and encourages it.

Countless commercials advise us, "You deserve a break today"; "Do your own thing!"; "Buy the best: You're worth it"; "If it feels good, do it." There are those like Bertrand Russell who have written books in praise of laziness and others who have written songs advocating it.

The Bible, on the other hand, encourages us to discipline ourselves for the purpose of godliness (1 Tim. 4:7), to endure hardness as a good soldier of Jesus Christ (2 Tim. 2:3), and to exercise self-control in all things (1 Cor. 9:25). The sluggards written about in the Bible are the original couch potatoes—happy to remain in bed long after they really need sleep (Prov. 26:14).

The Women's Health Initiative, a recent landmark study of 93,700 women, found that women who walked briskly one-half-hour daily five times a week cut the risk of heart disease by 30 percent.[3] In fact, regular exercise of any type lowers blood pressure and cholesterol, keeps weight down, and improves mental outlook.[4]

INTELLECTUAL

So far, we have really only considered the *physical* aspects of laziness. What about *intellectual* laziness? This is exactly what my husband (a college professor) has always deplored in his students. It is that tendency to accept superficial answers, to fail to dig below the surface, to neglect to ask questions, to avoid taking initiative. When was the last time you read a challenging and significant nonfiction book instead of some fluffy, lightweight work of fiction?

In *Candles in the Dark*, Amy Carmichael wrote, "It matters a good deal that your book-food should be strong meat. We are what we think about. Think about trivial things or weak things and somehow one loses fibre and becomes flabby in spirit."[5] In spite of heavy responsibilities, Charles Spurgeon was known to be an avid reader who devoured half a dozen "meaty" books in a week.[6] And John Wesley once said to a group of ministers: "Gentlemen, if you do not read, get out of the ministry."

Scientists today encourage older adults to exercise their brains. Pittsburgh neurologist Paul Nussbaum, addressing the National Council on Aging and the American Society on Aging, stated: "When you don't eat, you see the results on your body. When you don't learn, you can't see the damaging results, but trust me, it's the same."[7] He went on to suggest several activities that encourage a lifetime of brain growth and, if continued, can often help stave off dementia and other brain diseases of old age. These activities include learning a second language, exercise, gardening, learning to play a musical instrument, prayer, public speaking, and participating in organized choral singing.

I teach Bible study classes in which women are expected to do homework. The questions they have to answer before being allowed to participate in a discussion group are sometimes quite challenging.

But then, have you ever learned anything truly worthwhile without putting in some effort? I marvel at how many women come into Bible study after years of attending church with a remarkably shallow knowledge of the Bible. They have not been encouraged to love God's Word with their *minds* as well as their hearts. Thankfully, it is never too late to start.

Do you magnify obstacles and thus keep yourself from trying new things? Do you make excuses like, "I could never take college classes at my age," or "I could never write a book or learn a musical instrument at this late stage of my life." Haydn wrote his oratorio *The Creation* after age sixty-seven. Tennyson, at eighty-three, wrote "Crossing the Bar." Victor Hugo wrote *Les Miserables* when he was sixty-two, and Bible commentator Thomas Scott (1747-1821) began studying Hebrew at age eighty-seven. One characteristic of the sluggard is a tendency to avoid activity by magnifying imaginary obstacles. The sluggard says, "There is a lion outside; I will be killed in the streets!" (Prov. 22:13). Making much of nothing is a great excuse to sit back and *do* nothing.

SOCIAL

Laziness also has *social* ramifications. In later years, as your energy level declines, it is easy to view hospitality as "too much fuss" and to allow relationships of long-standing to dwindle and die by virtue of neglect. Proverbs 27:10 reminds us, "Do not forsake your own friend or your father's friend."

Our family has precious memories of older folks in their seventies and eighties who invited our family—including the children—for meals. It did not have to be fancy. One dear couple always insisted on having us over when we were in town. Even if we arrived with little advance warning, our hostess would go out for fast food, if need be. We would then sit down with nothing but hamburgers and perhaps some sliced tomatoes or peaches on paper plates. Who cared? We were richly blessed and would not have traded those visits for a seven-course meal.

Forget the elaborate rituals. If you lack the time and energy to prepare a full meal, invite someone over for dessert. Hospitality is so important that church leaders who neglect it do not meet the biblical qualifications for leadership (1 Tim. 3:1-2; Titus 1:5-8).

SPIRITUAL

What about *spiritual* laziness? Even Christians, who more than others pride themselves on having the right spiritual priorities, can become spiritually lazy in later years. We can coast along on what we learned years ago instead of breaking new ground. Are there sections of your Bible with hardly any notes in the margins—books you have never studied in depth?

Noted commentator Matthew Henry once wrote, "We shall not only be called into account for the truth that we knew and did not apply, but for the truth we might have known and did not come to know." Do you take adequate time to prepare for Sunday school classes and to prepare your heart for worship? Is prayer a habit of life as natural as eating three meals a day?

We all struggle in these areas. Conscious effort is needed to fight the prevalent habits of laziness in our society. The Virtuous Woman is one who "does not eat the bread of idleness" (Prov. 31:27). She stands in contrast to the wicked, lazy slave Jesus spoke of in the Parable of the Talents, who was unprepared for his Lord's return (Matt. 25:26). "Shun laziness," Voltaire said. "It is a rust that attaches itself to the most brilliant metals."

For Further Thought . . .

1. Describe your own philosophy for balancing work or other productive activity with rest and relaxation. Would you be comfortable having your friends know how you spend your leisure time? Explain.

2. Do a study of the sluggard in the book of Proverbs. Then list some of the typical characteristics of a sluggard.

3. Ephesians 5:16-17 teaches us to redeem (make the most of) our time because the days are evil. Read those verses and explain on a practical level how to apply them.

4. What effect will it have on you and others if you are lazy and uncommitted in maintaining relationships with other believers?

5. To Timothy, Paul wrote, "Discipline yourself for the purpose of godliness" (1 Tim. 4:7). How does discipline promote godliness? Are you in the habit of disciplining yourself? How?

Living for Pleasure

The abuse of a harmless thing
is the essence of sin.

—A. W. TOZER

" She who gives herself to wanton pleasure is dead even while she lives" (1 Tim. 5:6). It is to *widows* that the Bible directs these words. Such a widow, comments Donald Norbie, "is physically alive, but spiritually dead. What an indictment!"[1]

Lest you think that the merry widow of New Testament times reflects a lifestyle that afflicts only females, King Solomon in a much earlier era experimented with living for pleasure and found it wanting. He tried sensual and aesthetic amusements. He accumulated seven hundred wives and three hundred concubines, constructed architectural wonders, amassed great riches, and pursued scientific and philosophical interests. With the power and the money to indulge his every whim, he withheld nothing from himself. Nevertheless he discovered that "the eye is not satisfied with seeing, nor is the ear filled with hearing." In the end, he concluded that it was all vanity. "There is nothing new under the sun" (Eccl. 1:8-9).

Hedonism is the philosophy that pleasure is the principal good and should be the aim of our actions. Hedonism is a way of thinking that makes the self-indulgent pursuit of pleasure the highest priority. Today there exists a trend in some Christian circles to re-define hedonism in an attempt to make it acceptable—to talk about "Christian hedonism," as if that were not an oxymoron. What does living for pleasure have in common with "take up your cross daily and follow Me"? (Luke 9:23).

J. I. Packer labeled the drift toward hedonism in Christian circles, "hot tub religion." In a book on this subject, he wrote, "We have recast Christianity into a mold that stresses happiness above holiness, blessings here above blessedness hereafter, health and wealth as God's best gifts, and death, especially early death, not as thankworthy deliverance from the miseries of a sinful world . . . but as the supreme disaster, and a constant challenge to faith in God's goodness. Is our Christianity now out of shape?" He concluded, "Yes."[2]

It is not that God begrudges us pleasure. God Himself is the fountain of all true joy. The pleasures of life that He brings our way enhance our love for

God and appreciation of Him. There is no question that God delights to give us pleasure. The Bible tells us that He richly supplies us with all things to enjoy, that in His presence is fullness of joy, and at His right hand there are pleasures forever (1 Tim. 6:17; Ps. 16:11). The pleasures of life become a curse, however, when they grow to be the objects and focus of life instead of the evidences of God's lovingkindness. Jesus rebuked the scribes and Pharisees for (among other things) living lives full of "self-indulgence" (Matt. 23:25).

In his last letter, the apostle Paul made a dire prediction that "in the last days" people would become "lovers of pleasure rather than lovers of God" (2 Tim. 3:1-4). How does this happen? How does our focus swing away from God and shift to pleasure? Is this, too, something we are increasingly prone to as we age?

The short answer is "yes," probably because we have too much money and too much free time. Young married couples lack both the time and the money to indulge a love of pleasure. They are busy providing for the necessities of life and raising a family. In later life, however, we have had an opportunity to accumulate more assets. Then, with retirement, we face many choices about how we will spend our time and money. Perhaps we should bear in mind what our mothers told us long ago: "Idle hands are the devil's workshop."

Living for pleasure can take many forms. It may be as socially acceptable as watching television all day. It may be looking for sexual intimacy outside of marriage. Increasingly, even in Christian circles, older couples attempt to justify living together without benefit of marriage on the economic ground that it would adversely affect their incomes. The Bible has a word for sexual relations outside of marriage: It is called *immorality* (or *fornication* in the King James Version). Scripture strongly condemns it (1 Cor. 5:9-11; 6:9-11). Disobedience can be costly.

Money complicates the problem of too much leisure time. Before the current level of prosperity in our nation, choices for retirement were limited. Now, on the other hand, we may have the freedom to travel endlessly, to get a second vacation home elsewhere, or to buy a boat and spend our weekends cruising.

Many undesirable consequences follow from our pleasure-seeking. One is that church commitments and attendance become irregular. We lack accountability. In addition, how can we volunteer to teach a class or be available to help with even minimal responsibilities if we are off traveling or indulging our thirst for pleasure every third or fourth week? How can someone serve as an elder or deacon if he is absent from church for much of the year, spending weekends playing golf, boating, or enjoying frequent trips to Disney World and the Grand Canyon?

Saying "no" to such a lifestyle takes determination and discipline in a society that encourages self-indulgence, especially when we have the money to satisfy our desires. There is a place for recreation. A vacation can be an important time for rest, relaxation, and recharging our spiritual batteries. But we were not put on earth to please ourselves. Jesus died for us "that they who live *might no longer live for themselves,* but for Him who died and rose again on their behalf" (2 Cor. 5:15, italics added). Have the words of Philippians 1:21, "For to me, to live is Christ," been reduced to a meaningless cliché for our present generation? Sadly, at the very time in life when our schedules are free enough to take on responsibilities serving the Lord, we may lack the inclination to do so.

Unfortunately, the choice of one partner in a marriage to pursue a life of pleasure can also crush the ministry of his or her mate. Through the years I have seen numerous women decline leadership training in women's Bible studies. Their children are grown and their schedules are free. They now have the time and opportunity to develop their spiritual gifts—to participate with women who are learning such skills as how to effectively lead a discussion group, how to lead someone to faith in Christ, how to disciple, how to use Bible study tools, and how to become better organized. So what is a typical reason for their inability to do so? "My husband is retiring and would like me to be free to travel this year."

It would surprise many young people of our generation to know that "retirement" is a relatively new concept. Two hundred years ago, hardly anyone "retired" in the modern sense of the word.[3] In Puritan times, church elders routinely served for life. They rarely resigned and hardly ever retired. While retirement can bring many benefits, it actually is not an inalienable right covered under the Constitution! Neither are vacations.

Vacations, too, can bring a welcome time of rest, refreshment, reflection, and even a time for spiritual ministry. But the idea that we "need" or "deserve" a vacation, and that we cannot function optimally without one, is an idea that would have been laughed at in previous generations. Millions of people have lived and died without going on vacation! Dr. A. W. Tozer, to name one, did not believe in vacations and never took one, yet his life was astonishingly fruitful for the Lord.[4]

As the second verse of an old hymn puts it:

Work, for the night is coming,
Work through the sunny noon;
Fill brightest hours with labor—
Rest comes sure and soon.
Give ev'ry flying minute
Something to keep in store;
Work, for the night is coming,
When man works no more.

—ANNIE L. COGHILL 1836-1907

For Further Thought . . .

1. How does money complicate our choices in retirement? Have you ever held back from a major purchase (such as a boat or second home) for spiritual reasons—even though you could have afforded it?

2. Although the Pharisees were reputed to be pious religious leaders, Jesus condemned their hypocrisy and accused them of being *inwardly* filled with self-indulgence (Matt. 23:25). Do you think Jesus would draw similar conclusions about Christians and their lifestyles today? Comment.

3. For a time, King Solomon chose to live for pleasure. What did he conclude at the end of that period of his life? (Eccl. 2:1-11)

4. How does the love of pleasure *wage war* against our souls? (1 Peter 2:11; James 4:1-3)

5. During the past year, how have *your own* choices to travel for non-essential reasons impacted your level of commitment at church?

"The Cup Is Half Empty" Syndrome

There is a lot to be thankful for, if you take the time to look. For example, I'm sitting here thinking how nice it is that wrinkles don't hurt.

—AUTHOR UNKNOWN

People filter the experiences of life through different lenses. Most of us have a way of looking at life which our friends and family quickly identify: We see the cup of life as half full, or we are members of the-cup-is-half-empty group. Bible commentator Matthew Henry, who lived in the seventeenth century, must have belonged to the-cup-of-life-is-half-*full* group. Once, after being robbed of his wallet, he wrote this about the incident in his diary:

Let me be thankful, first, because he never robbed me before; second, because although he took my purse, he did not take my life; third, because although he took all I possessed, it was not much; and fourth, because it was I who was robbed, not I who robbed.

In contrast, how many of us after losing a wallet would still be worrying, complaining, and dramatizing "the event of the lost wallet" a week later, allowing it to produce headaches, anxiety, and lost sleep? (Though we must admit, life is more complicated these days, what with the hassle involved with getting re-issued credit cards, etc.)

Eeyore is the classic symbol for the-cup-is-half-empty syndrome. Remember Eeyore from the *Winnie-the-Pooh* books? He was the gloomy old gray donkey who responded to upbeat greetings of "Good morning, Eeyore," with words such as, "If it is a good morning, which I doubt. Not that it matters," and who made comments like: "Nobody cares. All is lost."

There is a reason my husband has several Eeyore coffee mugs! He knows he has to watch himself; he has a tendency toward depression which requires discipline and determination to overcome. How about you? Are you prone to looking at life through negative glasses? Since experts tell us that people over sixty are more prone to depression than any other age demographic, we obviously need to be on guard in our attitude toward life.

Stress comes in new forms as we age. We may still

worry about our children, even though they are grown. (We just add grandchildren to the list!) We may also struggle with financial matters. In addition, we face a continual stream of changes—retirement, declining physical strength, memory lapses, loss of independence, chronic health issues, and so on. It is easy to lose perspective, to focus on our problems, and to sink into negativism, anxiety, or self-pity.

The Bible addresses these concerns in a variety of ways—first, by telling us to change our focus! In Scripture, the Christian life is often compared to a race, and we are told to fix our eyes not on our problems, but on Jesus, who stands at the finish line, the author and perfecter of faith. That, we are told, is the antidote for growing weary and losing heart (Heb. 12:1-3). Charles Spurgeon said, "We must use our eyes with resolution, for they will not go upward to the Lord of themselves, but they incline to look downward, or inward, or anywhere but to the Lord."

Such focus requires disciplined thinking. Speaking at a conference, Paris Reidhead once said, "You were wired for victory at Calvary. After you find the switch, the issue is whether you *want* victory." The apostle Paul wrote to the Christians in Colossae about the need for a new focus: "If you have been raised up with Christ, keep seeking the things above, where Christ is, seated at the right hand of God. *Set your mind on the things above*, not on the things that are on earth" (Col. 3:1-2, italics added).

A change of focus goes a long way toward

preventing the murmuring and complaining that so often accompanies the aging process. As our aches and pains increase, so does our love of rehearsing the details to friends and family! We treat grumbling and complaining as trivial and unimportant sins, if we think of them as "sins" at all. The Bible reminds us, however, that those who grumbled in the wilderness lost their lives in judgment. Their story is reviewed in the New Testament as a warning and is "written for our instruction" (1 Cor. 10:10-11).

A change of focus also involves cultivating an attitude of thanksgiving, gratitude, and contentment, hard as that may be at times. When we face the losses associated with old age, Psalm 73:25-28 gives us a different way of looking at life: "Whom have I in heaven but You? And besides You, I desire nothing on earth. My flesh and my heart may fail, but God is the strength of my heart and my portion forever. . . . As for me, the nearness of God is my good."

Paul wrote to the Philippians, "I have *learned* to be content in whatever circumstances I am" (Phil. 4:11, italics added). Contentment does not come naturally; it must be learned. It demands disciplined thinking and prayer. Fortunately, Philippians chapter 4 provides concrete instructions for what we can do to gain "the peace of God, which surpasses all comprehension" and which will guard our hearts and minds in Christ Jesus (Phil. 4:7).

When we give free rein to negative thoughts, not only are we unpleasant to be around, but our thoughts tend to spill over into self-pity. Self-pity, in turn, exaggerates and dramatizes our circumstances. We start thinking like the prophet Elijah, who during a bout of depression complained to God, "I *alone* am left; and they seek my life, to take it away" (italics added). God gently reminded Elijah that thousands of people in Israel still had not succumbed to the worship of Baal (1 Kings 19:14-18).

When at a similar low point, we should remember that our problems are not unique, and that God will not allow us to be tested beyond our ability to endure them (even if it does not always *feel* that way). A great verse to memorize is 1 Corinthians 10:13:

> "No temptation has overtaken you but such as is common to man; and God is faithful, who will not allow you to be tempted beyond what you are able, but with the temptation will provide the way of escape also, so that you will be able to endure it."

The most significant times of spiritual growth in my own life have often been surrounded by adversity and painful experiences—such as the death of my granddaughter. We draw close to God at those times and seek to understand His ways. We learn new things about God's character, come to experience His peace, and are reminded that what happens in this life is only a small slice of eternity.

Ecclesiastes chapter 7 makes a strong case for the benefits of adversity:

"It is better to go to a house of mourning than to go to a house of feasting, because that is the end of every man, and the living takes it to heart. Sorrow is better than laughter, for when a face is sad a heart may be happy. The mind of the wise is in the house of mourning, while the mind of fools is in the house of pleasure. It is better to listen to the rebuke of a wise man than for one to listen to the song of fools" (Eccl. 7:2-5).

How strikingly this passage stands in contrast to the world's focus on fun and laughter as the highest good. Even in Christian circles, we see churches devoted to "holy laughter" and Christian comedy clubs. Although there is a time to laugh (as Ecclesiastes also teaches) and to be refreshed by the joyful and pleasurable experiences God brings into our lives, when we make them an end in themselves, they destroy right priorities and usurp the place of God.

To fully appreciate the sovereignty of God is to realize that nothing happens to us which has not first been filtered through His hands. He allows experiences we may find difficult and unpleasant for a purpose. Ecclesiastes 7:14 reminds us, "In the day of prosperity be happy, but in the day of adversity consider—God has made the one as well as the other." In the mean time, "A joyful heart is good medicine, but a broken spirit dries up the bones" (Prov. 17:22).

For Further Thought . . .

1. What were some sources of stress in the apostle Paul's life that could have easily resulted in depression? See, for example, 2 Corinthians 1:8-10.

2. List the things you learn from Philippians 4:4-13 that could help to guard us from depression and discouragement. From verse 11, discuss how one "learns" to be content.

3. Why is sorrow often better for us than laughter, according to Ecclesiastes 7:1-4? Read this passage from the Bible in at least two or three different translations.

4. According to a recent study, "Seniors are the highest risk population in the country for suicide."[1] What factors may contribute to this statistic?

5. How can we best minister to elderly friends who experience significant losses and are prone to depression?

6. What verses in the Bible help you the most when the stresses of life incline your heart toward self-pity and discouragement?

Breakdown in Relationships

Some Christians are like porcupines. They have many fine points, but it's hard to get next to them.

—Vance Havner

One of my sons, while still a teenager bagging groceries at a local supermarket, developed a negative attitude toward older people. There he had the chance to observe numerous cranky, demanding, and fault-finding elderly folks. Sour-faced and quick to complain, they seldom offered a smile or a thank-you for this complimentary service. His attitude was reinforced while mowing lawns for older people. He once described an elderly woman who stretched a string between her yard and her neighbor's yard and watched carefully to make sure that my son did not cut one blade of grass on the wrong side of the string!

At one time, our family lived next door to a retired minister who loved to grow roses. Unfortunately, the elderly woman who lived behind him complained vigorously that the rose petals which dropped off his aging roses fell over the fence into her yard and onto her grass! Today our family uses the phrase "rose petals on the lawn" as a byword for obsessing over trivial issues of life. Young people might say to such a person, "Get a life!" There are certainly better ways to spend our time and energy.

What makes people that way? What would your next-door neighbors say about you? Busy and productive people do not usually have time to fixate on "rose petals on the lawn." Even in old age, when energy levels decline to the point where ministries outside the home become difficult, there are meaningful ways to keep busy—writing encouraging notes, talking with a neighbor, spending meaningful time in prayer—activities that matter in light of eternity.

The one who lacks solid goals and possesses too much free time may obsess about trivial matters. Does getting older make it more likely that we will fall into such patterns? If so, what can we do about it? Perhaps you have observed (as I have) a loss of social inhibitions in people as they age. It seems as if defects that were uncorrected in youth become concentrated and more prominent in old age. If a woman had a critical spirit when she was young, it often seems more pronounced in old age. If a man obsessed about money when young, he may do so even more late in life.

In *Caring for Those Who Can't*, Carol Dettoni writes: "In old age, people become what they have always been, only more so."[1] Revelation 22:11, a difficult verse, seems to imply that choices we make over time become our fixed character in old age: "Let the one who does wrong, still do wrong; and the one who is filthy, still be filthy; and let the one who is righteous, still practice righteousness; and the one who is holy, still keep himself holy."

Can you think of other habits that, when uncorrected, worsen in old age? Those who have a tendency to worry in their youth may become chronic worriers in old age. Those who are hypochondriacs when young may be a sore trial to their caregivers when old. The list goes on. All of these negative characteristics strain relationships with family and friends. They also can lead to loneliness, as others no longer enjoy spending time with them.

Although neurological reasons may contribute to the loss of social inhibitions, much of the behavior we engage in is under our control and has spiritual roots. How important it is to identify and work on spiritual shortcomings while we are young, before they become ingrained habits. President Theodore Roosevelt said, "Old age is like everything else; to make a success of it you've got to start young!" One of my own goals is to keep working on that "gentle and quiet spirit" which is precious in the sight of God

(1 Peter 3:4). That is one area where effort is still needed on my part.

Change contributes to the stress of life as we age. Someone has said, "Blessed are the flexible, for they shall not be bent out of shape." One church leader made these observations about the inflexibility of the elderly in church life:

> Younger Christians are not immune to conflict. But more often, in my experience, it has been the older ones who succumb to the temptation of demanding things go their way. Resistant to change, some view anything new as liberal, suspicious, or from the devil.[2]

Have we become too used to getting our own way? Do we need to be reminded about the doctrine of mutual submission taught in Ephesians 5:21? When was the last time you held a strong opinion on some non-essential issue (such as changing the color of the carpet, or the times of church meetings), and you yielded without a fuss?

On the other hand, resistance to change is not always bad, and indeed may be a vital function of older people, especially in the church. The experience of having grown up in a different era at a different time can give us a perspective and an objectivity about our current culture which serves as an important anchor to prevent detrimental changes. The Bible warns us not to be swayed by every new wind of doctrine (Eph. 4:14). Thus, providing that it is *reasoned*, resistance to change by the older members of a congregation can function as an important part of the "immune system" for the body of Christ.

Related to unreasonable inflexibility may be unwillingness to yield authority. Once someone has been in leadership, used to wielding authority and influencing others, it is hard to step down and cede decision-making to others. Even after doing so, the temptation arises to manipulate events from the sidelines and to undercut those newly chosen for positions of leadership. Some churches take the easy way (but not the scriptural way) out and adopt a mandatory age when elders must step down because, left to themselves, leaders may refuse to drop the reins. Power is seductive. One virtue of the shared leadership advocated by the New Testament is that it provides peers who can influence the decision to step down.

Talking too much is another trait which, when uncorrected in youth, becomes a greater liability in old age. It can, again, lead to a breakdown in relationships with friends and family. Memory lapses may add to the problem, as we keep telling the same stories, unmindful of our repetitions. Are there people you avoid engaging in conversation because they talk too much and rarely listen? Do you mentally groan when you hear a certain voice on the telephone? Dale Evans must have believed that this trait worsens in old age because she suggested these verses as part of an Elderly Person's Prayer:

Lord, keep me from the habit of thinking I must say something on every subject and on every occasion.

Keep my mind from the recital of endless details—give me wings to get to the point.

I ask for grace to listen to the tales of others' pains with patience. But seal my lips on my own aches and pains.

With my vast store of wisdom, it seems a pity not to use it all—but Thou knowest that I want a few friends at the end.

—FROM DALE EVANS, *TIME OUT, LADIES*[3]

Anyone familiar with the Bible knows that it has much to say about the tongue and the need to control it. Consider some of the following:

* ❋ "If anyone thinks himself to be religious, and yet does not bridle his tongue but deceives his own heart, this man's religion is worthless" (James 1:26).
* ❋ "He who restrains his lips is wise" (Prov. 10:19).
* ❋ "He who restrains his words has knowledge" (Prov. 17:27).
* ❋ "A fool's mouth is his ruin, and his lips are the snare of his soul" (Prov. 18:7).
* ❋ "He who guards his mouth and his tongue, guards his soul from troubles" (Prov. 21:23).

These verses are just a small sample of the emphasis the Bible puts on guarding our speech. A trouble-making woman once told John Wesley, "God has given me the talent of speaking my mind." Mr. Wesley snapped back, "God wouldn't mind if you buried that talent."

One of my favorite verses is Proverbs 12:23: "A prudent man *conceals* knowledge" (italics added). That verse frees me from thinking I must say something on every subject—even if I have the answer! There is a time in life to do more listening, to draw others out, and to ask the questions that will help *them* to think, rather than routinely giving the answers.

We have already considered several qualities that can damage relationships in our later years: a negative, sour attitude; obsession over trivial matters; lack of flexibility; unwillingness to yield authority or to adapt to change; and talking too much. One trait, however, looms especially large in the breakdown of relationships in old age: failure to forgive. We have a natural tendency to minimize our own sins and maximize the faults of others. A long life gives us a long time to store up memories of past hurts that have never been truly resolved. We hurt ourselves when we nurse old grudges and keep the memory of old wounds alive by failing to forgive.

John MacArthur writes that early in his pastoral ministry he discovered that most of the problems which led people to seek counseling were related to issues of forgiveness.[4] A tendency to be a grudge-bearer when we are young, if uncorrected, will be worse in old age. Unless the Lord harnesses our tongues and controls our attitudes, we will be more apt to tell someone off, to refuse to forgive, and to be satisfied to sit alone and sulk, alienated from friends and family. Hasty words can kill relationships of long standing.

Unresolved anger leads to unforgiveness. Although the Bible makes it clear that anger is not necessarily wrong, it must be kept in bounds and dealt with scripturally. We read in Ephesians chapter 4:

> "Be angry, and yet do not sin; do not let the sun go down on your anger, and do not give the devil an opportunity. . . . Let no unwholesome word proceed from your mouth . . . and do not grieve the Holy Spirit of God. . . . Let all bitterness and wrath and anger and clamor and slander be put away from you, along with all malice. Be kind to one another, tender-hearted, forgiving each other, just as God in Christ also has forgiven you" (Eph. 4:26-32).

Notice the warning against *bitterness*. We read in Hebrews 12:15, "See to it that no one comes short of the grace of God; that no *root of bitterness* springing up causes trouble, and by it many be defiled" (italics added). Roots grow below the surface where they can hide and do their damage unseen. Botanists affirm that many plant diseases are spread by root contact. Are you careful to pull out any roots of unforgiveness in the soil of your own life? Someone has said, "To forgive is to set the prisoner free . . . and then discover the prisoner was you."

For Further Thought . . .

1. What changes occur in later life that promote stress and may lead to inflexibility? Are there ways we can guard against stubbornness and a refusal to accept change?

2. When is resistance to change a bad thing? When is it a good thing? Discuss some of the changes that are taking place in the churches in this generation.

3. It seems incredible that those who profess to be followers of the Lord Jesus Christ sometimes hold long-standing grudges, even refusing to speak to fellow-believers for years. How serious is it to fail to forgive? (Matt. 6:12-15; 18:21-35; Mark 11:25; 1 Cor. 11:27-30; Heb. 12:15).

4. Have you ever stepped down from a position of authority and watched as another person took your place? When changes occurred, were you tempted to meddle from the sidelines? *Did* you?

5. What kind of habits have you observed in people that tend to worsen in old age? Have you identified a problem area in your own life? What are you doing to correct it?

Botox and Facelift Choices

*Some people, no matter how old they get,
never lose their beauty—they merely move it
from their faces into their hearts.*

—Martin Buxbaum

In November 2005, *U.S. News and World Report* informed us that "78 million baby boomers are approaching retirement age, and many of them have no intention of looking the part."[1] According to the article, consumers spent $6.4 *billion* dollars on anti-aging skin products in 2004, an increase of 21 percent from the previous year. One Botox injection, used to paralyze facial muscles and diminish the appearance of wrinkles, costs between $300 and $600. In 2004 alone, more than two *million* Botox injections were given. And that does not include such things as laser treatments, dermal fillers, and thermage, a deep-skin treatment using radio frequency which costs up to $2,000 per treatment.[2]

Obviously, appearance has become big business. As our society moves increasingly toward a youth-oriented culture, having a youthful appearance is perceived as essential for business and social success. In the nineteenth century, cosmetics were associated primarily with prostitutes and aristocrats.[3] In the twentieth century, they have not only become accepted, but are often considered necessary for success.

In the Christian community, change is also taking place. When our parents or grandparents were young, it was considered scandalous for a woman to dye her hair. If she did so, it was not discussed in public. Today there are probably more professing Christian women who dye their hair than those who do not do so. And change is not confined to women. Men are also increasingly dyeing their hair, getting hair transplants, using toupees to cover baldness, and seeking other remedies to prolong the appearance of youth.

Debate among Christians on such issues is not confined to our own time, either. Spurgeon wrote that "Mr. Wesley was stigmatized as eccentric because he wore his own hair when all the fashionable world rejoiced in wigs."[4] Spurgeon himself was denounced by a Dutchman who abandoned his good opinion of Spurgeon and his writings after seeing him in person. Why? Because, according to Spurgeon,

I wore a beard, which was bad enough, but worse than this, he observed upon my lip a *moustache*! Now this . . . he might have overlooked. . . . But no, he said that I wore a moustache like a carnal, worldly-minded man! Think of that! Instead of being all shaven and shorn like the holy man whom he was accustomed to hear, and wearing a starched ruffed collar all around my neck, about a quarter of a yard deep, I was so depraved as to wear no ruff, and abjure the razor.[5]

Such issues easily become a bone of contention in Christian circles. How should we respond to today's all-consuming emphasis on one's looks? I was in my upper teens when I became a Christian believer, and I wanted to be a godly woman. But I remember looking around at some older Christian women and thinking, "Do I have to look like *that* to be godly?" The appearance of so many of them was unappealing and outdated. I tried "looking spiritual" my freshman year of college and wore no make-up. My roommates decided I "looked like the devil" (their very words!) with no make-up. It was not the image I wished to cultivate!

Do Christians have to look dowdy? Is it wrong to want to look nice? Is it possible to go from one extreme to another? When the prophet Samuel went to anoint the next king of Israel, he was warned not to be swayed by looks. The Lord reminded him that, "God sees not as man sees, for man looks at the outward appearance, but the LORD looks at the heart" (1 Sam. 16:7). That verse provides some needed balance. It teaches that if we want to please God, focusing on the heart is the higher priority. However, the verse also reminds us that "man looks at the outward appearance." We live in the world of people who *cannot* see our hearts and who may be attracted or repelled by our appearance.

Christians have many differing ideas on what constitutes worldliness in dress and appearance. Some Christian women believe eye make-up is wrong but surreptitiously use a little concealer, powder, or blush. Some think wedding rings and watches are acceptable, but not earrings. Opinions about hair and dress are equally diverse. Is it okay to curl, tease, and style your hair, but not to dye it? Is a nonsurgical facial skin peel acceptable, but not a facelift? You get the picture!

We make so many of these decisions based on what we see around us. It is almost impossible to step back from our own culture and from the way we were raised to examine these issues dispassionately. Do we even think to consult God? Then again, even when we look at specific cases in the Bible, it can still be difficult to make decisions. If we condemn eye make-up because wicked Queen Jezebel wore it (2 Kings 9:30), must we then approve of nose rings because good Rebekah, wife of Isaac, had a nose ring? (Gen. 24:47).

Whatever individual decisions we make before the Lord, the Bible neither promotes nor condones excessive time and attention being given to our looks. Do we spend as much time in spiritual pursuits as we do trying to be physically attractive? In Isaiah's time, God's stinging rebuke of the women of Jerusalem calls attention to their frivolous, worldly life-style centered on external beauty. They

> ". . . walk with heads held high and seductive eyes, and go along with mincing steps and tinkle the bangles on their feet. . . . The Lord will take away the beauty of their anklets, headbands, crescent ornaments, dangling earrings, bracelets, veils, headdresses, ankle chains, sashes, perfume boxes, amulets, finger rings, nose rings, festal robes, outer tunics, cloaks, money purses, hand mirrors, undergarments, turbans and veils. . . . Instead of a belt, a rope; instead of well-set hair, a plucked-out scalp; instead of fine clothes, a donning of sackcloth; and branding instead of beauty" (Isa. 3:16-24).

The New Testament instructs women not to let their adornment be merely external but to dress modestly, discreetly, and appropriately (1 Tim. 2:9; 1 Peter 3:3). How, then, are we to apply these verses in making specific decisions? Issues beside vanity may influence our practice. One author wrote, "The determination of a woman of age to appear young is not born of vanity, but the knowledge that power lies in youth."[6] Reality tells men and women that in some cases looking "too old" may cost them their jobs or keep them from getting one.

We need principles to help us make decisions that will please God in the gray areas. By *gray areas* I mean the choices in life we make which do not seem to be covered by specific commands in Scripture. No verse tells us that getting a monthly pedicure is a sin, or that Botox injections are a good idea. Leaving aside the economic and health/safety issues of those choices, God has given us principles to apply in any given situation. Here are some to think about when making decisions about your physical appearance in the gray areas:

First, be mindful that your body does not belong to you (1 Cor. 6:19-20). Christians have been bought with a price, the blood of Christ. Their *bodies* have an eternal purpose and will one day be renewed, transformed, and raised up (Phil. 3:21). If our bodies belong to God, doesn't He have the right to be consulted about these decisions? Second, whatever we do is to be done to the glory of God (1 Cor. 10:31). Is the choice you have in mind consistent with God's presence in your life? Does it help show others what God is like? If known, would it hurt your reputation in the Christian community in which you function?

Perhaps most important is the third principle: Do not violate your own conscience. After seeking God's will in prayer, you should be convinced in your own mind that you are doing the right thing (Rom. 14:5). If in your heart you think it is wrong, for you it is wrong! "Happy is he who does not condemn himself in what he approves. . . . Whatever is not from faith is sin" (Rom. 14:22-23). If your attitude about something is highly defensive ("Why *shouldn't* I?") and secretive (afraid to tell your friends you are getting a facelift?), chances are that you are already offending your own conscience.

Finally, realize that you are an individual and your choices need not always conform to those around you. In the celebration of holidays, for example, Paul wrote, "One person regards one day above another, another regards every day alike. Each person must be fully convinced in his own mind" (Rom. 14:5-6). If you have a heart that genuinely desires to please God, He will guide you to make the choices that are pleasing to Him.

In her book *Getting Over Getting Older*, Letty Pogrebin writes, "I'm interested in figuring out what makes certain women appealing into their sixties, seventies, and eighties."[7] I have seen that special beauty in the faces of some older women. It is nothing that beauty treatments can buy. Perhaps the world needs to meet more such people who have focused on inner beauty. They are comfortable with their aging bodies and not trying to look like teenagers in their sixties and seventies.

If some day you make the decision to "go gray," the Bible contains these encouraging words: "A gray head is a crown of glory; it is found in the way of righteousness" (Prov. 16:31).

For Further Thought . . .

1. How have views on what constitutes "acceptable" clothing in Christian circles changed in your own lifetime? Were these good changes? Bad changes?

2. What are some of the principles you would suggest for deciding how a person can look attractive without falling into worldliness, immodesty, or inappropriate clothing?

3. If money were no object, would you get a facelift? Botox injections? A hair transplant? Other forms of body-sculpting? Why or why not?

4. How may a person's physical appearance affect the way we treat them—even in Christian circles? (See James 2:1-4.) What is the remedy for this?

5. How does "looking old" affect us in the workplace? Should this influence the choices we make about our appearance?

6. With less energy in old age, we easily become careless about hygiene and clothing. *Why* do we need to guard against this? *How* can we guard against this?

Walking with the Lord

Christian funeral directors provide many valuable services, but they can't phone ahead for reservations—you must apply in person for Eternal Life.

—Church announcement board in
New Brighton, Pennsylvania

As a friend and I ate lunch together one day, we began to discuss the foibles of our parents. She was concerned about her mother's new passivity toward life. Her mother, now in her late sixties, seemed to be withdrawing more than could be explained by the state of her health. A new mask had settled over her character. Although she managed to get out for church on Sunday, she was less communicative and seemed to lack the initiative needed to cultivate relationships with others.

I shared some of my own experiences. For eleven years we had our parents living with us—first my husband's parents, and then my own. For a short time, until the first one died, we had all four of them under our roof! In those days it seemed that we were running our own assisted living facility. We had time to observe some of those foibles ourselves and to think about a few areas we want to watch closely in our own lives as we grow older.

One such area is our relationship to God. The Bible tells us that the righteous "will flourish like the palm tree. . . . They will still yield fruit in old age" (Ps. 92:12-14). How can we be sure that we will be still bearing fruit and walking with the Lord at the end of our lives? And what does the phrase "walking with the Lord" really mean?

On the surface, "walking with the Lord" sounds like a cliché without much meaning. However, dozens of verses in the Bible tell us how to walk. We are to "walk by faith, not by sight." We are to "walk in love," to "walk honestly," and to "walk in the light." Walking becomes an idiom for how we live our lives, moment by moment and step by step. It speaks of consistency.

What about "walking" spiritually in our old age? One author has written, "Old age is like a minefield; if you see footprints leading to the other side, step in them."[1] We have such footprints. The Bible speaks of believers walking in the steps of Abraham, that great man of faith (Rom. 4:12). David wrote of the person who has the Word of God in his heart: "His steps do not slip" (Ps. 37:31). But walking *with the Lord* is even more to the point. Jesus said, "He who follows Me will not walk in the darkness, but will have the Light of life" (John 8:12). How does a person come to have a real relationship with God which makes that possible?

In my own case, while growing up I do not recall ever hearing my parents pray, nor can I think of a time when the Bible was read in our home. My parents, however, would have considered themselves Christians. As far as they were concerned, if you were not Jewish, by default you were a Christian. My parents were also socially conscious, and since all good people sent their children to church, they selected an appropriately prestigious church in our community (complete with velvet-padded kneeling benches and stained glass windows) and sent us there to Sunday school.

I grew up in that environment—baptized as a baby, winning awards in Sunday school, going through confirmation in my early teens, and, by the time I was in high school, teaching a class of pre-school children. I was no great skeptic, but I do remember looking out my bedroom window at night, sometimes saying my prayers, and wondering if there really was a God up there who was listening. I never knew there was anything more to the Christian faith than that. I never knew a person could actually come to know God in personal experience and could have the assurance of eternal life promised in the Bible to believers (1 John 5:13).

In high school, a friend invited me to a Christian camp. There I heard the gospel clearly explained for the first time in my life. I understood my need for salvation and the sufficiency of Jesus Christ to meet that need. It was a message that demanded an individual response. I prayed and asked the Lord Jesus Christ to come into my life as my Savior. On that day (August sixth), I wrote, dated, and signed these words in my Bible:

> I am, as a lost sinner, willing to receive Jesus Christ as my personal Savior, believing that He was God's Lamb, that He took my place when He died on the cross and that His shed blood was a sufficient atonement for my sin. I am willing to confess Him before men as my Savior.

The transformation of my life began—rather slowly at first—and has continued since that time. Scripture tells us that coming to know God personally is the essence or core of genuine Christianity. Jesus said, "*This* is eternal life, that they may *know* You, the only true God, and Jesus Christ whom You have sent" (John 17:3, italics added). I learned that there is a vast difference between knowing *about* God and knowing Him personally.

If a person is deceived about his or her relationship with the Lord, the stakes are very high. As we age and draw closer to the finish line, it is all the more important to be clear about our relationship to God. Some who expect to get into heaven may be cherishing a false hope. Being active in church or observing the rituals of church life does not guarantee a pleasant afterlife. As someone has said, "A passion for God is not to be confused with a passion for the things of God."[2] You may think that you know God, but does He know *you*? Jesus taught that

> "Not everyone who says to Me, 'Lord, Lord,' will enter the kingdom of heaven; Many will say to Me on that day, 'Lord, Lord, did we not prophesy in Your name, and in Your name cast out demons, and in Your name perform many miracles?' And then I will declare to them, '*I never knew you*; depart from Me, you who practice lawlessness'" (Matt. 7:21-23, italics added).

New life begins with birth. This is as true of spiritual life as it is of physical life (John 3:3, 7). My own spiritual life really began in my teens, but it is quite possible to be an eighty-one year old baby who has just begun a relationship with the Lord (as was true of my father-in-law). After birth, a process of spiritual growth is to be expected in an eighty-one-year-old as well as an eighteen-year-old. Neither spiritual nor physical growth is automatic. We neglect it at our peril. Scripture tells us that we should, like a newborn baby, long for the pure milk of the Word of God (1 Peter 2:2). It also instructs us not to neglect our fellowship with other believers

(Heb. 10:25) or with the Lord Himself (1 Cor. 1:9).

Times of prayer can blossom in later years. How good to know that we can pray at any time, day or night, sick or healthy, lying down or standing up. Minimal calories are burned; little physical energy is expended—yet prayer is probably the hardest thing we do. We long to get down to the business of the day. Our lists of activities are long, and our energy may be limited. Am I the only one who feels as if I do not pray enough? Who struggles with wandering thoughts? Who is easily distracted? Who sometimes does not *feel* like praying? An old Puritan prayer, part of which contains these words, speaks to my heart:

> O Lord, I have a wild heart and cannot stand before thee. . . . I neglect prayer, by thinking I have prayed enough and earnestly, by knowing thou hast saved my soul. Of all hypocrites, grant that I may not be an evangelical hypocrite, who sins more safely because grace abounds."[3]

Late in life and with fewer demands on our time, we have increased opportunity to deepen our relationship with God, to be quiet before Him, and to study the Bible in a leisurely and meditative fashion. Find the method and the time that works best for you. For years I felt guilty hearing of those great saints of the past who rose at four in the morning for two hours of prayer and Bible study. Studying the Bible first thing in the morning has seldom worked well for me. I have joked with friends that I study the Bible the way a snake eats: many snakes tend to eat one big meal about once a week. The majority of my Bible study is done on one day set aside for that each week.

Reading from a short devotional booklet is no substitute for real Bible study. There is a place for Bible *reading* (such as reading through the Bible in a year), but that, too, is not Bible *study*. Real Bible study takes significant effort, and it is not just for preachers and those involved in full-time Christian ministry. Elders are commended for "working hard" at preaching and teaching, reminding us that Bible study can indeed be hard work (1 Tim. 5:17)!

Paul wrote to Timothy, "Be *diligent* to present yourself approved to God as a workman who does not need to be ashamed, accurately handling the word of truth" (2 Tim. 2:15, italics added). He told Timothy not to neglect his spiritual gift, but to "take pains" with these things, so that his "progress will be evident to all" (1 Tim. 4:14-15). It would be interesting to ask our friends and fellow-believers if our progress in the Christian life—even into old age—is evident to them.

Finally, we can think of "walking with God" as a metaphor for friendship. The Bible says that "Enoch walked with God," and one day God just scooped him up and took him to heaven without dying! Enoch pleased God (Heb. 11:5). Just as a person must take the initiative in building or strengthening a human friendship, so we need to take initiative to strengthen our relationship with God. When we do not spend time with friends, the relationship cools, and so it is with God. Do not wait for Him to tap you on the shoulder.

For Further Thought . . .

1. To a non-Christian friend, how would you explain the difference between knowing about God and actually knowing Him personally?

2. What are some factors that might contribute to spiritual passivity in old age? Are you in better spiritual shape now than you were ten years ago?

3. Is there a difference between (1) reading the Bible; (2) studying the Bible; and (3) having your devotions? If so, do we need to practice two of them? All three?

4. Both Zacharias and Elizabeth, even in old age, are described as "walking blamelessly" in the sight of God (Luke 1:5-7). Discuss the idiom of "walking" with the Lord. What kind of "walking" characterizes your own life?

5. What opportunities do older Christian men and women have to be spiritual role models to younger believers? (Titus 2:2-5).

18

Maintaining Accountability

*Being accountable to someone means you sit
face to face, look that person in the eye and
honestly, openly discuss what is going on in
your lives.*

———Jim Clayton

D aniel Webster was once asked, "What is
the greatest thought that has ever entered
your mind?" He replied, "My accountability to
Almighty God." We are not reminded often
enough that "each one of us will give an
account of himself to God" (Rom. 14:12). In
the Parable of the Talents, Jesus taught that the
servants who were entrusted with gifts by the
Master will be called to account for their
stewardship when He returns (Matt. 25:14-29).

To be accountable is to be answerable, or
responsible, to another party. We are not
always happy to face that fact. Pontius Pilate
tried to avoid responsibility for handing Jesus
over to an angry mob that demanded His

crucifixion. Pilate washed his hands and claimed to be "innocent of this Man's blood." Words alone do not absolve us of responsibility. As the apostle Paul reminded the Corinthian Christians:

> "Each man's work will become evident; for the day will show it because it is to be revealed with fire, and the fire itself will test the quality of each man's work. If any man's work . . . remains, he will receive a reward. If any man's work is burned up, he will suffer loss; but he himself will be saved, yet so as through fire" (1 Cor. 3:13-15).

If we know that one day we will stand before God and be accountable to Him, why not practice accountability now? Christian fellowship provides a natural opportunity to be accountable to each other. Recall that the Greek word κοινωνια [koinonea], commonly translated *fellowship,* means *sharing.* We share our hearts, we share our burdens, and we share encouragement with one another. In a small church, for instance, where you are known to many or most of the people, if you are absent from a service on Sunday, you may get a telephone call asking if everything is all right. That is accountability!

Many today are uncomfortable with accountability. Our independent nature tends to reject the idea of being answerable to anyone. Pride and guilt are also factors. Perhaps we would be embarrassed having others know how we spend our time. Unfortunately, the laziness against which we all struggle is fostered by not being accountable.

What about those who avoid small group interaction and deliberately choose a large church where they can come and go with no one's scrutiny? Commandments like those in Hebrews 13:17, "Obey your leaders and submit to them, for they keep watch over your souls as those who will give an account," are widely ignored. By avoiding accountability we give our leaders precious little opportunity to keep watch over our souls.

In a landmark Harvard study on adult development and aging, good social supports which involved meaningful relationships were important factors of successful aging.[1] Another significant research project, the MacArthur Foundation Study, linked social relationships and social support to longevity, while demonstrating that social isolation is a powerful risk factor for poor health.[2]

Do you struggle with leading a disciplined life? Do you have problems being consistent with daily devotions? Do you really want to change? I double-dog-dare you to get into an accountability group! Accountability groups are especially important for those who may be retired, who live alone, or who are not in any kind of a structured Christian group that provides personal interaction and the needed incentive for disciplined prayer and Bible study.

How can you develop such a relationship? The first step toward accountability is to be in regular church attendance. Next, get into a worthwhile small group, such as a Sunday school class and/or a structured Bible study. A prayer partner can function as an accountability partner. "Two are better than one," wrote the Preacher in Ecclesiastes, "for if either of them falls, the one will lift up his companion. But woe to the one who falls when there is not another to lift him up" (Eccl. 4:9-10).

If, in order to lead a more disciplined life, you need more specific accountability, prayerfully consider choosing two to four discreet friends of the same sex with whom you are comfortable and form an accountability group. *Love* and *trust* are the necessary glue to make this relationship work; *pride* and *fear* are its chief obstacles. Pride may cause us to be less than candid about our weaknesses. Fear that we will no longer be loved if we expose our weaknesses may also inhibit candor. Set those fears aside and take the risk! The benefits far outweigh the risks.

One of the chief advantages of an accountability group is that it forces us to look at our lives more closely and to be aware of problem areas we might otherwise overlook. In forming such a group, make a commitment for six months. Then reassess whether all wish to continue the arrangement. Agree ahead of time that you will meet once a month and ask each other the hard questions, such as:

1. Did you have a prayer time each day this month?

2. How were you involved in ministering to others?

3. What kind of physical exercise did you do?

4. How much television did you watch? What did you do to fight laziness?

5. What conflicts did you get into? How were they resolved?

6. What did you study in the Bible this month?

7. What worthwhile new books or other material did you read?

8. How faithful were you in church attendance?

9. How responsible were you in financial matters?

10. What temptations were a particular problem for you?

11. What did you intend to do and never complete?

12. What are your specific goals for next month?

It bears repeating that chief among the hazards of old age are indolence and irresponsible self-gratification. One of the best defenses against these traits that suck the life out of spirituality is accountability. Those who function as our accountability partners can encourage us to be of service to God and to others. They can also help us not to retreat into ourselves to our own spiritual detriment.

Hardly anything works more effectively than a fellow believer suddenly looking you in the eye and pointedly asking, "How are things between you and the Lord?" or "What have you been studying in the Bible this week?"

For Further Thought . . .

1. How is accountability a part of your life? Would you profit by being in a more structured accountability arrangement?

2. Write a plan for setting up an accountability group. What ground rules would it have? How often would it meet? What questions would be asked?

3. What is the relationship between stewardship and accountability? (1 Cor. 4:1-4; 9:16-17; 1 Peter 4:10)

4. What kind of financial accountability was practiced by leaders of the New Testament church? (1 Cor. 16:1-4; 2 Cor. 8:20-21)

5. Do you think it is a good idea to employ your spouse as an accountability partner? Why or why not?

19

Setting Specific Goals

Most people would rather look backward than forward because it's easier to remember where you've been than to figure out where you're going.

——Anonymous

The very first verses in the Bible that I memorized—within two weeks after I became a Christian—were from Ephesians 2:8-10:

> "⁸ For by grace you have been saved through faith; and that not of yourselves, it is the gift of God; ⁹ not as a result of works, so that no one may boast. ¹⁰ For we are His workmanship, created in Christ Jesus for good works, which God prepared beforehand so that we would walk in them."

Many Christians have memorized verses 8 and 9. It is wonderful to know that salvation does not depend on us or our works but on God's grace, provided as a gift through faith exercised in Jesus Christ. But few focus on verse 10, which speaks of God's *purpose* in providing that salvation: we were created in Christ Jesus for good works. Even before we became believers, God had prepared good works that He intended us to do.

The apostle Paul apparently had some idea of the works that God intended *him* to do. Among other things, he realized that God planned for him to minister specifically to non-Jews (the uncircumcised) and to the poor (Gal. 2:7-10). Do you know what God's plans and purposes are for your own life? What "good works" has He planned for you to do? He has given each of us gifts and abilities that enable us to carry out those purposes, yet many believers continue for years with no clear idea of what their gifts are and how they are intended to use them.

Defining spiritual goals has nothing to do with seeking the limelight, as some suppose. In his book *No Little People, No Little Places*, Francis Schaeffer points out that setting goals does not mean seeking fame or glory. To be the Lord's servant is to take the lowest place unless God extrudes you into a position of greater responsibility and authority.[1] Kenneth Fleming echoes that concept in his book, *He Humbled Himself: Recovering the Lost Art of Serving*.[2] The words of Jesus are just as true today as they were 2,000 years ago: "The greatest among you shall be your servant" (Matt. 23:11). So, where can you serve?

Brother Lawrence (1608-1691), who peeled potatoes in a monastery kitchen for much of his life, wrote that "we ought not to be weary of doing little things for the love of God, who regards not the greatness of the work, but the love with which it is performed."[3] Never famous in his time, Brother Lawrence still enriches the lives of many today through the brief letters he wrote, known collectively as *The Practice of the Presence of God*. Written over 300 years ago and translated into numerous languages, they still provide counsel and encouragement for believers today.

According to a Harvard study on adult development and aging, the people who exemplify positive aging are those who cherish initiative.[4] They are open to learning and to seeking new interests in life. And so it is worth asking, what are your goals? Precisely what things do you still want to accomplish with your life? Sometimes it is worth writing down specific goals and looking at the list often. It has been said that many people have a good aim in life, but for some reason they never pull the trigger! Making those goals specific is a step in the right direction.

Caleb had a goal that motivated him for forty-five years: he wanted to possess the territory where his feet had walked when he spied out the Promised Land. He achieved that goal at age eighty-five! (Josh. 14:6-14). One of the apostle Paul's goals was to preach the gospel in new places where Christ was not yet known rather than building on another person's foundation (Rom. 15:20). Ezra, a scribe living after the Babylonian captivity, had a goal to return to Jerusalem. There he planned "to study the law of the LORD and to practice it, and to teach His statutes and ordinances in Israel" (Ezra 7:10). And so he did.

It is good to have some short-term goals and some long-term ones. A short-term goal of mine is to become more proficient using certain computer software. One teaching goal I have is to learn and teach something new each year that I have never taught before. How easy it is to continue to focus on the parts of the Bible that have become very familiar. It takes time and energy to conquer new territory, to study methodically, and to learn thoroughly. I have still another goal: to write inductive Bible study materials on the few books of the Bible that I have not yet completed.

And then there are personal and family goals. Do you have an authentic goal to get into better physical shape? What steps have you laid out to achieve it? Goals need to be both specific and realistic. A doctor friend of ours advises his overweight patients to lose only two pounds a month, not ten or fifteen. Being overly ambitious breeds discouragement when our goals are unmet.

Perhaps you plan to write out your life story, complete with pictures, for your grandchildren. A step in that direction—a mini-goal—might be to organize the hundreds of photographs you have taken without ever printing, labeling, or organizing them. Break that goal down further by planning to organize the first hundred or so pictures this week! Put it on the "to do" list for a specific day.

Once you are retired, your goals may include some short-term missionary work. With increased leisure time, you have the opportunity to try new things, to give your time freely to causes that have touched your heart. In *Setting Goals That Count*, Joseph Allison writes, "Develop your ability to serve God by exercising your availability, your dependability."[5] There are endless possibilities. If God were to tell you, as He told King Hezekiah, to "set your house in order" because you will soon die, what new goals would suddenly leap to the forefront of your attention?

My husband reported having a conversation with several students as they worked together in biology lab. He casually asked them what they would do if they knew they had only a short time to live. Most of their answers boiled down to "party like mad," "live it up," and "indulge myself." (This exchange took place at a secular college; hopefully the answers would be far different in Christian circles.) The students' answers reveal a philosophy distinctly opposite to that of biblical Christianity. Goals, whether major or minor, reflect our real orientation and aspirations toward life. Are we here to please ourselves or to glorify God?

In his book *Success Is a Choice*, Rick Pitino points out that "goals are our day-to-day blueprint that provide achievable targets. . . . They show us where to start and they establish our priorities. They make us organized and create discipline in our lives."[6] Pitino went on to say, "If you are not willing to work hard and establish discipline in your life, then all your dreams are merely going to be pipe-dreams."[7]

There is a big difference between dreams and goals. Many dreams and desires do not become goals. No plan is mapped out to achieve them. Truthfully, I have a desire to learn a great deal more Hebrew, but time constraints being what they are, I have as yet no concrete plan to make that desire an achievable goal.

In *The Eagle's Secret*, David McNally writes, "The great contributors in life often start with just a glimmer of what they might accomplish. But through consistent action, they fan the flame, celebrating even the smallest victories along the way."[8] The later years could turn out to be the most exciting and significant period of your life. Author George Eliot wrote, "It is never too late to be who you might have been!"

For Further Thought . . .

1. What are some goals that you have mapped out for the future? Have you broken them down into mini-goals? How?

2. Do you have any idea what some of the "good works" are that God has planned for you still to do? See Titus 2:14 and Ephesians 2:10.

3. What new *practical* skill would you like to learn within the next six months? How will you achieve that goal?

4. Late in life, after we have achieved many of our former goals, what reasonable goals might remain for us—even with diminished energy or abilities?

5. Contrast *worthy* goals with the kind of selfish ambition that can subtly infect our lives. See, for example, Judges 8:22-27; 3 John 9-10; and Philippians 1:14-17.

20

Choosing and Evaluating Activities

There cannot be a crisis until next week.
My schedule is already full.

—HENRY KISSINGER

Time management seems to be a problem at almost any age. Young couples today run from one frenzied activity to another, strung out, exhausted, and over-committed. Moms speak of living in their cars as they drive their children to sports practice, music lessons, or other obligations. Some operate under the illusion, "When I retire, I'll have lots of time." From what I hear, however, older people are busier than ever and frequently wonder how they had time to hold down a full-time job!

Even activities classified as "serving the Lord" can keep us busier than we were meant to be. I was still in my twenties when a wise, older Christian woman named Frances Lister gave me this advice: "Never forget that the *good* is the enemy of the *best.*" There are many "good" things we can do. Sometimes we are trapped into doing them because we are able, available, and have never learned to say "no." I took her advice and immediately dropped one "Christian" activity that had little significance in light of eternity. I have used Miss Lister's advice many times to weed out less important activities that sap time and energy from the best things I could be doing.

We were not meant to be running about like chickens with our heads cut off. In today's world, unfortunately, one's sense of worth and esteem are often tied to how we answer the question, "What do you *do*?" If you can spew out a long string of important activities—especially if they make lots of money—then you must really be *somebody!* Socrates warned his followers (and Christians have often quoted these words), "Beware the barrenness of a busy life." True, one can be too busy. On the other hand, according to a MacArthur Foundation Study of what constitutes successful aging, one factor that helps to define successful aging is continued involvement in productive activities.[1] So how, from a Christian point of view, should we define *productive?* We need to choose activities wisely and re-evaluate them often when energy levels decline in later years.

Some activities are necessities. They pertain to the everyday needs of life—shopping, cleaning, fixing, exercising, and so on. Others reflect pleasures of life that refresh us—leisure interests in art, music, hobbies, or other pursuits that enrich us in varying ways and often provide meaningful contacts and opportunities with those outside the Christian community. Leaving aside those two categories, what other activities should be on our priority list? What will matter one hundred or two hundred years from now? Jesus said,

> "Do not store up for yourselves treasures on earth, where moth and rust destroy, and where thieves break in and steal. But store up for yourselves treasures in heaven, where neither moth nor rust destroys, and where thieves do not break in or steal; for where your treasure is, there your heart will be also" (Matt. 6:19-21).

What might some of those treasures be that await us in heaven? We send our worship and our prayers ahead. Brother Lawrence wrote that "we ought to purpose . . . to become in this life, the most perfect worshipers of God we can possibly be, as we hope to be through all eternity."[2] Our prayers, too, are sent ahead to become part of the golden bowls of incense mentioned in Revelation 5:8 and 8:3.

What other treasures cannot be destroyed by moths, rust, decay, or thieves? The Bible makes it clear that two things in this present world are going to last into eternity: people and the Word of God.

People will continue to exist in one realm or another. Some "will go away into *eternal* punishment, but the righteous into *eternal* life" (Matt. 25:46, italics added). The Word of God will also exist forever (1 Peter 1:25).[3]

In making decisions about how best to serve the Lord *when we are older*, the Bible also provides some specific guidance for our choices. For example,

> "*Older* women . . . are to be . . . teaching what is good, so that they may encourage the young women to love their husbands, to love their children, to be sensible, pure, workers at home, kind, being subject to their own husbands, so that the word of God will not be dishonored" (Titus 2:3-5, italics added).

Understanding how to implement those instructions can often prove difficult. Unfortunately, the organizational structure of many churches works against carrying them out by segregating older women from younger women so that they are always in separate activity groups.

If older women are to be role models and teachers of younger women, it stands to reason that interaction between the two groups needs to be encouraged. Then, perhaps, young women will turn to older ones to learn how to love their husbands and their children instead of turning to dubious books on the subject or to their inexperienced peers.

Hopefully, those of you reading this who are older

Christian women have already given thought to the types of activities that give you opportunity to interact with young women. The benefits of your Christian experience can be passed on in both formal and informal ways. Have you come up with ideas, for example, on how to encourage young women to be "pure," to be "sensible," or to be "keepers at home"? Are you clear about what these words mean?

Older women can also learn what activities God esteems by studying the role of widows in 1 Timothy. Here we find what is expected of a widow over sixty-years of age who is considered worthy of the church's support. She is known for her hospitality, for being a woman of prayer, for assisting people in distress, and for devoting herself "to every good work" (1 Tim. 5:3-10).

The Bible also speaks to older men. They are to be "temperate, dignified, sensible, sound in faith, in love, in perseverance" (Titus 2:2). Older men also need to interact with young men. Their example is needed. The younger generation is watching! Do they see qualities in you such as perseverance—how you hold up under stress and disappointment? In the Greek language of the New Testament, the same word translated *older man* (πρεσβυτερος) is often translated *elder*. Context frequently requires that it refer to those who lead or rule in an assembly (1 Tim. 5:17; Titus 1:5). Aspiring to serve in that capacity is a worthy goal, according to Scripture (1 Tim. 3:1).

Finally, in your later years, think back on the

special ways you have served the Lord during your life. What have you learned? What knowledge and skills do you possess that you can pass on to the next generation before you die? The apostle Paul wrote to the Philippians, "The things you have learned and received and heard and seen in me, practice these things" (Phil. 4:9). I am strongly motivated to disciple others by what Paul, shortly before his death, wrote to his helper Timothy: "The things which you have heard from me in the presence of many witnesses, entrust these to faithful men who will be able to teach others also" (2 Tim. 2:2).

Note that the word translated "men" is the Greek word *anthropos* (ανθρωπος), meaning people in general—men and women, not just males. I take that to mean that the abilities to serve God I have gleaned through the years also need to be entrusted to faithful *women* of the next generation. Because of that, as opportunities arise, I teach other women how to lead someone to faith in Christ, how to disciple, how to lead a discussion group, how to study the Bible more effectively, how to manage their time more efficiently, or even how to cook. I believe God will hold me accountable for what I have learned.

You may be gifted at teaching or organizing. You may be great at planning retreats, camping, or working with teens. Perhaps you have gained victory over worry or depression. Maybe you have a special talent for encouraging young women who are trying to make it as single moms. Has God given you a sweet spirit while living with an unbelieving spouse? Allow God to use the victories you have won and the lessons you have learned to benefit the next generation. Choose activities and contacts with younger people that will enable you to do so.

In selecting activities, do not forget to choose at least one that will bring you into contact with those outside the faith. Many Christians fill their days exclusively with Christian activities. They become ingrown and out of touch with the non-Christian world, resulting in an inability (and perhaps a lack of desire) to effectively share their faith with unbelievers. To avoid this pitfall, think about volunteering for a worthwhile charity or similar organization that will give you needed interaction with those outside your own circle of faith.

For Further Thought . . .

1. Do a Bible study on *treasures.* How do we lay up treasures in heaven? What does it mean to be "rich toward God" (Luke 12:21)? Also see Matthew 6:19-21 and 19:21.

2. List at least two or three abilities you have which would benefit those younger in the faith. What is the best way to pass them on to the next generation?

3. What activities are you currently involved in that bring you into contact with non-Christians and could provide the opportunity to share your faith with them?

4. Who has helped train and encourage you spiritually? Who has passed on to you the skills that have been most helpful in your Christian life?

5. Comment on Miss Lister's advice: "The *good* is the enemy of the *best.*" Are you presently involved in "good" activities only because you never learned to say "no"? Are they draining energy from those which are more important in light of eternity?

PART

4

*Drawing on
God's Grace*

Dealing with Loss, Healing, and Disease

While we are in this tent, we groan, being burdened.

—2 Corinthians 5:4

Therefore, being always of good courage . . .

—2 Corinthians 5:6

We are of good courage, I say, and prefer rather to be absent from the body and to be at home with the Lord.

—2 Corinthians 5:8

Granted, we groan . . . but are we always of good courage? That's the hard part. And although we don't talk much about courage, the Bible certainly does. We need courage for many things. Getting old is not for sissies. Commentator Albert Barnes wrote, "It is not improper for a man who sees old age coming upon him to pray for special grace to enable him to meet what he cannot but dread." That's realism for you! Without courage there will be times when we are tempted to wallow in self-pity.

A friend wrote me that while walking past a bookstore, she spotted a little book titled *All the Good Things About Getting Old*. Thinking of my writing project, she immediately opened the book and found nothing but blank pages! That produced a hearty chuckle. Are there good things about getting older? Is successful aging an oxymoron? The MacArthur Foundation Study of Successful Aging included freedom from disease and disability as important components of successful aging.[1] Must Christians have the same perspective? Must we be unhappy if we are unhealthy?

The other side of the equation is Proverbs 15:15: "All the days of the afflicted are bad, but a cheerful heart has a continual feast." Attitude influences everything! Christians were designed to experience joy and laughter. Proverbs 17:22 reminds us, "A joyful heart is good medicine, but a broken spirit dries up the bones." In *Laugh Again*, Charles Swindoll writes, "People who live above their circumstances usually possess a well-developed sense of humor."[2] He advises, "Find Christian friends who see life through Christ's eyes, which is in itself . . . encouraging. Have fun together. Share funny stories with each other. Affirm one another."[3]

God does not minimize the losses and sorrows of old age, but He does provide compensations and comfort: "Even to your old age and gray hairs I am he, I am he who will sustain you. I have made you and I will carry you; I will sustain you and I will rescue you" (Isa. 46:4, NIV). "We do not lose heart," the apostle Paul wrote. "Though our outer man is decaying, yet our inner man is being renewed day by day" (2 Cor. 4:16).

Certainly, hard challenges accompany aging. Over time we face many losses. We may lose status after stepping down from a position of prominence. We lose friends and relatives who die. Later we may lose hearing, muscle strength, memory, coordination, balance, bladder control, and so on. It goes without saying that each of these is a difficult adjustment. Losses may impinge on our ability to drive a car, to experience sexual intimacy, to live independently, or to maintain privacy. Is it possible to maintain a steadfast, uncomplaining spirit in all this?

The oldest known text on the sorrows of old age was produced in 2500 BC by the Egyptian poet Ptahhotep. He wrote, "How hard and painful are the last days of an aged man . . . The power of his mind lessens and today he cannot remember what yesterday was like. All his bones hurt."[4] The oldest book in our own personal library was written by William Bates, a Puritan, and published in 1691. In it he wrote, "The union between soul and body is very intimate and dear, and . . . they part unwillingly."[5]

Diminished physical capabilities need not cripple our productivity. Cicero (106-43 BC) wrote, "It is not by muscle, speed, or physical dexterity that great things are achieved, but by reflection, force of character, and judgment; in these qualities, old age is usually not only not poorer, but is even richer." College professors observe that older students often do much better than those just out of high school. They may have a tougher time memorizing, but they are motivated, disciplined, and determined to succeed—and they do. The Talmud teaches, "For the unlearned, old age is winter; for the learned, it is the season of harvest."

Perhaps the greatest challenge of aging is facing serious illness. In her book *Encounter with Terminal Illness*, Dr. Ruth Kopp writes:

> We . . . fear that we will find ourselves unable to bear the burden of a serious illness and prove not to be as strong as we had hoped we were. . . . What if the illness uncovers my own peculiar area of cowardice, vanity, or fear, and I am not able to withstand it?[6]

Christians at such times naturally turn to God in prayer and to fellow believers for support. Even today God answers prayer and heals miraculously. Scripture encourages us to pray for good health and for healing (3 John 2; James 5:14). Asa, one of the kings of Judah, began his reign well but finished badly. In the thirty-ninth year of his rule he became severely "diseased in his feet." Yet we read that when he was sick, "he did not seek the LORD, but [only] the physicians."[7]

Praying about illness and seeking divine healing, however, do not mean ignoring medical help or medicinal remedies. Jesus assumed the validity of seeking medical help when He said, "It is not those who are healthy who need a physician, but those who are sick" (Matt. 9:12). God may choose natural or supernatural means to heal.

But what if He does not heal? Reasons for sickness and other physical problems may be hidden from us. Job's illness, long a mystery to himself, stemmed not from sin, as his "comforters" claimed, but from a situation that arose between God and Satan (Job 2:1-7). Paul's infirmity worked to keep his ego from being inflated (2 Cor. 12:7-9). Physical problems may be the result of sin (Ps. 32:1-5; 1 Cor. 11:28-30; 1 John 5:16-17) or the abuse of our bodies. Still others may be designed specifically to bring glory to God in some unique way (John 9:1-3).[8]

Illness may also come simply because it is our time to die. Beware of those who point to "lack of faith" as the reason you do not experience healing. Faith must be anchored in the will of God. We seek to understand that will (1 John 5:14-15). The prophet Elisha, a man of enormous faith, was sick in bed and died of a fatal illness—yet he was still exercising faith and performing miracles for others from his sick bed (2 Kings 13:14-20). In His divine wisdom, God chose not to heal him.

Dr. Ruth Kopp points out that God sometimes heals instantaneously, without medical intervention. Other times He allows disease, pain, and suffering. She goes on to say that

. . . those who prove the quality of their faith by refusing all medical attention and by clinging to the unswerving belief that God alone will heal them are as likely to die of cancer or another disease as anyone else. . . . Spiritual pride in our own faith and presumption of our understanding of . . . God's complete will are real dangers here.[9]

In the absence of healing, Dr. Kopp points out, there is also the danger of denial, resulting in "a frantic pilgrimage from doctor to doctor . . . from one revival to another, from faith healer to faith healer." Such a person may then turn to "quack remedies, special diets, and other 'cures' reported in the press."[10]

The apostle Paul performed many miracles and healings (Acts 15:12; 28:8) but left his fellow-worker Trophimus sick at Miletus, apparently without being able to heal him (2 Tim. 4:20). Paul's helper Ephaphroditus was sick "to the point of death" but apparently recovered gradually without any evidence of instantaneous, supernatural healing (Phil. 2:25-28). Paul himself prayed three times for his own healing, but the Lord said "no" (2 Cor. 12:8-9).

In his classic commentary on the gospel of John, J. C. Ryle wrote, "Health is a great blessing, but sanctified disease is greater. Prosperity and worldly comfort are what we all naturally desire; but losses and crosses are far better for us, if they lead us to Christ."[11] A clear understanding and acceptance of the sovereignty of God can provide us peace of heart regardless of circumstances.

The night before His crucifixion, Jesus said to His disciples, "These things I have spoken to you, so that *in Me* you may have peace. In the world you have tribulation, but take courage; I have overcome the world" (John 16:33, italics added). The peace Christ gives is supernatural: "Peace I leave with you; My peace I give to you; not as the world gives do I give to you. Do not let your heart be troubled, nor let it be fearful" (John 14:27). Do you have sure knowledge that the Lord Jesus Christ is your Savior? That peace is available to you now. Isaac Watts expressed it well in this verse taken from his Hymn 83:

> *Not all the pains that e'er I bore*
> *Shall spoil my future peace,*
> *For death and hell can do no more*
> *Than what my Father please.*[12]

These words by Isaac Watts remind me of a Bible verse that used to bother me. Have you ever encountered a Bible verse that really stuck in your craw? I once wrestled—agonized—complained— about this verse: "*No harm* befalls the righteous, but the wicked are filled with trouble" (Prov. 12:21, italics added).[13] I complained to the Lord: How can that verse possibly be true? Don't bad things happen to righteous people all the time? Don't Christians get mugged, robbed, and ripped off? Don't they get sick and suffer?

The answer is: of course they do! But nothing can harm the real you—the essence of who you are. God's plans for you are made in light of eternity. Job knew that even though worms might destroy his body, yet in his flesh he would see God (Job 19:26). Can anything separate us from the love of Christ? Can tribulation or distress or persecution or famine or nakedness or peril or sword? "In all these things we overwhelmingly conquer through Him who loved us" (Rom. 8:37).

The apostle Paul wrote to the Philippians, "I have suffered the loss of all things" (Phil. 3:8). But in a later paragraph of the same letter he wrote, "Rejoice in the Lord always; again I will say, rejoice! . . . Be anxious for nothing, but in everything by prayer and supplication with thanksgiving let your requests be made known to God. And the peace of God, which surpasses all comprehension, will guard your hearts and your minds in Christ Jesus" (Phil. 4:4, 6-7).

For Further Thought . . .

1. Why is courage needed when facing loss and disease? Where can we get it? How do we access it? What do the following verses teach us about courage: Joshua 1:6, 7, 9, 18; Mark 15:43; John 16:33; Acts 23:11 and 18:15?

2. To whom should we go when seeking to be healed—faith healers or the elders of the church? See James 5:13-16. What do you think these verses mean?

3. Losses can produce loneliness and isolation. What things can be done to minimize the isolation experienced by those who lose mobility and cannot drive? How can we best minister to them?

4. Some studies indicate that people of faith live longer and healthier lives than other people do. How does faith affect health and longevity? What might be some reasons for this?

5. Comment on J. C. Ryle's statement that "Health is a great blessing, but sanctified disease is greater." Practically speaking, how can that be?

6. Why do Christians facing terminal illness sometimes turn to unproven diets, bizarre remedies, and quack medicines? How should we respond when we see Christian friends moving in this direction?

"When My Trophies at Last I Lay Down"

Jesus, my only hope Thou art,
Strength of my failing flesh and heart;
O, could I catch a smile from Thee,
And drop into eternity!

—CHARLES WESLEY

Charles Wesley, at age eighty, dictated the above lines of this, his last hymn, after pondering these words from Psalm 73:

"Whom have I in heaven but You? And besides You, I desire nothing on earth. My flesh and my heart may fail, but God is the strength of my heart and my portion forever. . . . As for me, the nearness of God is my good" (vv. 25-28).

What will it be like to "drop into eternity," as Wesley put it? Do Christians suffer and die the way non-Christians do? Many years ago I put that question to our family physician, who was both a Christian and a family friend. His answer intrigued me. He said, "Unfortunately, Christians often suffer just as much as unbelievers. They may lose their mind, behave irrationally, and say and do things they would never do in their right mind. But they don't die the same way. It can be an awe-inspiring experience to be present when a Christian dies. I believe they sometimes see angels. One can often sense a Presence in the room."

Dr. Diane Komp was not a Christian when she first became a pediatric oncologist. But the way she saw some children die drew her to consider the claims of Christianity. In *A Window to Heaven* she writes about the case of Anna:

> Today many children with leukemia are cured, but this was not the case when Anna first became sick. Her therapy brought her periods of time when she was disease-free . . . but she faced the end of her life at age seven. Before she died, she mustered the final energy to sit up in her hospital bed and say: "The angels— they're so beautiful! Mommy, can you see them? Do you hear their singing? I've never heard such beautiful singing!" Then she laid back on her pillow and died.[1]

Certain aspects of death and dying mystify us. Even Christians who are old and in poor health may look on the end of life with mixed feelings. The Bible calls death an *enemy*—the last enemy that will be abolished (1 Cor. 15:26). When sin entered the world, it brought the penalty of death and the accompanying consequences of sickness, pain, and suffering. If we are secure in our relationship with God and confident of eternal life, will we still be afraid when the time comes?

Fear of death is natural. Billy Graham wrote, "It is not a sign of weak faith for the Christian to face death with reluctance."[2] In the Psalms, during a time of great stress, David wrote, "My heart is in anguish within me, and the terrors of death have fallen upon me. Fear and trembling come upon me, and horror has overwhelmed me" (Ps. 55:4-5). Yet as he ended the psalm, he came to this conclusion: "Cast your burden upon the LORD and He will sustain you; He will never allow the righteous to be shaken" (Ps. 55:22).

We have certain God-given instincts for survival that make it difficult to let go of life. Interestingly, our last days on earth may be likened to a woman in labor. In fact, Jesus uses that analogy to answer questions about the end of the age in Matthew 24:7-13. The birth pangs that women experience are no fun. But think how lovely it was to look into the eyes of your newborn baby for the first time. Now think what it will be like to behold the Lord Jesus Christ face-to-face for the first time—to see the glories of heaven and to be united with loved ones. Is there any question about it being worth it all?

The fear a Christian feels as death approaches is

probably more about the *process* of getting there than what awaits us on the other side. How will we hold up under suffering? (You women will understand: Will I scream and embarrass myself when I am in labor?) The answer is that God's grace is always sufficient (2 Cor. 12:9). You do not need dying grace until you are dying! One thinks about martyrs like the Reformer John Hus, who was burned at the stake. He wondered how he would hold up when the flames touched him, but he died singing.

One reason God took on human flesh and went through the experience of death was to "free those who through fear of death were subject to slavery all their lives" (Heb. 2:14-15). For Christians, "Death is swallowed up in victory." The sting of death has been removed (1 Cor. 15:54-57). When Christians walk through the valley of the shadow of death, they fear no evil, because the Lord is with them (Ps. 23:4).

For the non-Christian, on the other hand, fear of death can be crippling. Death is "the king of terrors" for those who do not know God (Job 18:14, 21). The writer of Hebrews states, "It is appointed for men to die *once* and after this comes judgment" (Heb. 9:27, italics added). "Once" reminds us that there is, in reality, no such thing as reincarnation—a philosophy which fosters the idea that we will always have another chance. Decisions in this life determine where we will spend eternity. For unbelievers, "It is a terrifying thing to fall into the hands of the living God" (Heb. 10:31).

What, then, constitutes a "good death?" Barbara Deane writes,

> If there is a Christian attitude toward death, I believe it's not to escape death (for this is impossible), nor is it to make a quick exit so we can maintain the illusion of controlling our own destiny. . . . I believe a good death, when one has had time to prepare, is one in which a person is ready to leave this earth because he feels his work here is completed. He can move on to the next world without regret because no "unfinished business" is tying him to this one.[3]

When Hezekiah became mortally ill, the prophet Isaiah came to him with a message from the Lord: "Set your house in order, for you shall die and not live" (Isa. 38:1). The purpose of this book is not to discuss all the practical arrangements of life that need to be made as one gets closer to the finish line (many books exist on that subject), but to remind us of the need to take care of any unfinished business before that time comes. What do you need to do to "set your house in order"?

If you are the caregiver for an aging parent or other relative, your help is desirable in such matters too. Family members need to be prepared to "let go" of those who are ready to die. Be there to listen. Do not shut them up when they want to talk about dying, even if it is hard for you to listen. "Unfinished business" may involve repentance toward God or attempts at reconciliation with estranged relatives and former friends. It may also entail making medical decisions to forego future medical treatment, sharing parting words with loved ones, or determining how assets should be allocated.

Perhaps you have seen the bumper sticker, "He who has the most toys at the end wins." A bumper sticker challenging that belief states, "He who has the most toys at the end still dies." Our grandparents used to put it this way: "There are no pockets in a shroud." The Bible pointedly reminds us, "For we have brought nothing into the world, so we cannot take anything out of it either" (1 Tim. 6:7). The hymn "The Old Rugged Cross" contains this memorable chorus:

> *So I'll cherish the old rugged cross,*
> *Till my trophies at last I lay down;*
> *I will cling to the old rugged cross,*
> *And exchange it some day for a crown.*[4]

I can only guess what "trophies" hymn writer George Bennard had in mind when he penned those words. When I think of trophies that will be laid down, I think of garage sales and estate sales, common in my part of Florida. Spread out on tables are the "stuff" of life, after the relatives have picked over the valuable possessions—trinkets, awards, diplomas, knick-knacks. I wonder which of my own treasures, perhaps precious because of sentimental value, will be on those tables some day, picked over by disinterested strangers. In the end, "Only what's done for Christ will last."

Right up until the last breath we draw, we can glorify the Lord Jesus Christ. I love the verses in Romans that state, "For not one of us lives for himself, and not one dies for himself; for if we live, we live for the Lord, or if we die, *we die for the Lord*" (Rom. 14:7-8, italics added). To the Philippians, Paul expressed his desire that "Christ will even now . . . be exalted in my body, whether by life *or by death*" (Phil. 1:20, italics added).

Aristeides, a Greek writing about AD 125, tried to explain the Christian religion to a friend: "If any righteous man among the Christians passes from this world, they rejoice and offer thanks to God, and they escort his body with songs and thanksgiving as if he were setting out from one place to another nearby." And so they are.

Until that time comes, "Let us run with endurance the race that is set before us, fixing our eyes on Jesus, the author and perfecter of faith" (Heb. 12:1-2). In *Send* Magazine, K. P. Yohannan writes,

The secret of our survival is fixing our eyes on Jesus and making Him alone our focus. Then our walk with God and our commitment to serve Him will no longer depend on whether or not people treat us right or circumstances are in our favor. We will no longer rely on our emotions to support us or on our successes to keep us going. Jesus alone will become our goal and motivation—our prize—and we will live for Him, run our race for Him, and cross the finish line for Him.[5]

It seems fitting to end this chapter, as well as this book, with the doxology. Many are familiar with the third verse, but few know all three original verses. Below is the *complete* doxology, also known as "The Evening Hymn" by Thomas Ken (1637-1711):

Teach me to live, that I may dread
The grave as little as my bed;
Teach me to die, that so I may
Rise glorious at the judgment day.

O may my soul on Thee repose,
And may sweet sleep mine eyelids close,
Sleep that may me more vigorous make
To serve my God when I awake.

Praise God, from whom all blessings flow;
Praise Him, all creatures here below;
Praise Him above, ye heavenly host;
Praise Father, Son, and Holy Ghost.

"For all of God's true children," wrote A. W. Tozer, "there will be another chapter, a chapter that will begin with the resurrection and go on as long as eternity endures."[6]

For Further Thought . . .

1. When you think of leaving things behind after your death, what "trophies" come to mind?

2. Romans 14:8 states, "If we die, we die for the Lord." On a practical level, explain what this really means.

3. Do you fear death? What is it you fear most of all? Discuss your own feelings about death.

4. Joseph Addison (1672-1728) wrote, "See in what peace a Christian can die." Have you been present when a loved one died? Share some of the things you learned from that experience.

5. The subject of euthanasia is widely discussed in the media. Is there a difference between *helping* someone die (2 Sam. 1:5-16) and *letting* them die (Prov. 31:6)? What does the Bible teach on this subject?

6. What kind of "unfinished business" needs to be addressed before you are ready to let go of this life?

Endnotes

Introduction

1. James L. Snyder, *In Pursuit of God: The Life of A. W. Tozer* (Camp Hill, PA: Christian Publications, 1991), 122.

Chapter 1. Good News / Bad News

1. David Hackett Fischer, *Growing Old in America* (New York, Oxford UP: 1977), 6.

2. John Langone, *Growing Older: What Young People Should Know About Aging* (Boston: Little, Brown & Co., 1991).

Chapter 2. The Purpose of the Aging Process

1. Robert E. Ricklefs and Caleb E. Finch. *Aging: A Natural History* (New York: Scientific American Library, 1995), 140.

2. Jay Olshansky, Bruce Carnes and Butler Butler. "If Humans Were Built to Last" in *Scientific American* (March 2001), 51.

3. Leonard Hayflick, PhD. *How and Why We Age* (New York: Ballantine Books, 1994), 266.

4. Ibid, 267.

Chapter 3. Some People in the Bible and How They Aged

1. While it is true that death entered the world because of sin (Rom. 5:12), the Bible makes it clear that not all diseases or ailments have a direct link to specific sins. See, for example, John 9:2-3 and 2 Corinthians 12:7-9.

Chapter 4. What Is Happening to My Body?

1. Letter of Susanna Wesley to her son John, written in 1727.

2. Charles R. Swindoll. *Living on the Ragged Edge* (Waco, TX: Word Books, 1985), 351.

3. Other translations say, "desire fails," but the Hebrew word seems to refer more precisely to the caperberry, which was believed to stimulate both appetite and sexual desire. See *Gesenius' Hebrew-Chaldee Lexicon*.

Chapter 5. Making Hard Choices: Paul, Abraham, Moses

1. Credit is due here to Howard Hendricks. Although this is probably not an exact quotation, I heard him make similar statements (while speaking at a dinner I attended) about the percentage of those in the Bible who did not finish their lives well.

2. Genesis 12:4. Acts 7:2-4 makes it clear that God first spoke to Abraham while he lived in Ur. Abraham moved first from Ur to Haran in Mesopotamia, then from Haran to the Promised Land.

3. Read more about the fascinating excavations at Ur in Chaldea. Leonard Woolley, *Ur of the Chaldees* (New York: Norton, 1965).

4. Deuteronomy 4:33; Exodus 33:11, 18-23; 34:29-35.

Chapter 6. Overcoming Obstacles: Joseph, Sarah, Daniel

1. It is likely, but not a certainty. Note the word *eunuch* used in most translations of Isaiah 39:7 and 2 Kings 20:18. The same Hebrew word is used seven times in Daniel 1. Castration was widely practiced on palace servants to prevent any sexual involvement with the ruler's harem.

Chapter 7. Praying Always: Samuel and Anna

1. E. M. Bounds, *Essentials of Prayer* (New Kensington, PA: Whitaker House, 1994), 11-12.

Chapter 8. Snared by Worldliness: Noah and Demas

1. Read her touching story in *A Foxfire Christmas*, ed. by Eliot Wigginton (New York: Doubleday, 1990).

2. Discussed by Josephus in his *Antiquities* (XVI. vi. 5).

3. *John Wesley's Notes on the Old and New Testaments,* commenting on Genesis 6:9.

4. See, for example, Habakkuk 2:15; Genesis 19:31-36; 2 Samuel 11:13; 13:28; and Leviticus 10—note verses 9-10 in connection with the deaths of Nadab and Abihu.

5. Sally K. Rigler, "Alcoholism in the Elderly." *American Family Physician* (March 15, 2000): 61,6. <www.aafp.org/afp/20000315/1710.html>.

6. See also 1 Timothy 3:3; 1 Corinthians 11:21; Luke 21:34; Ephesians 5:18.

Chapter 9. Snared by Sex: David and Solomon

1. David Hackett Fischer, *Growing Old in America* (New York: Oxford UP, 1977), 44.

2. Deuteronomy 17:15-19; 1 Kings 11:3.

3. Statistics from the Centers for Disease Control and Prevention (CDC), May 5, 2007. <http://healthlink.mcw.edu/article/1031002371.html>.

Chapter 10. Pride Goes Before a Fall: Miriam and Uzziah

1. See the entry for Numbers 12:1 in *Matthew Henry's Commentary on the Whole Bible.*

2. For Saul's disobedience, see 1 Samuel 13:9-14; for Uzza's, see 2 Samuel 6:3-7, which is explained by Numbers 4:5-6, 15; 7:8-9; for Aaron's sons, see Leviticus 10:1-3.

Chapter 11. Rejecting Wise Counsel: Joash and Amaziah

1. Read the fascinating story of Joash in 2 Kings 11-12 and 2 Chronicles 22-24.

Chapter 12. Taking It a Bit Too Easy

1. From "Come, Thou Fount of Every Blessing" by Robert Robinson (1735-1790).

2. Melvin Maddocks, "Let's Hear It For Decrepitude," *New York Times,* Aug. 27, 1999.

3. *U.S. News and World Report,* vol. 140, no. 8, March 6, 2006, p. 68.

4. *Time Magazine,* vol. 167, no. 26, June 26, 2006, p. 73.

5. Amy Carmichael, *Candles in the Dark* (Fort Washington, PA: Christian Literature Crusade, 1996), 3.

6. Bob L. Ross, *A Pictorial Biography of C.H. Spurgeon* (Pasadena, TX: Pilgrim Publications, 1974), 101.

7. *St. Petersburg Times*, March 13, 2005, p. 3A.

Chapter 13. Living for Pleasure

1. Donald L. Norbie, *1 Timothy: Timeless Truths for Today's Church* (Kansas City, KS: Walterick Publ., 1991), 100.

2. J. I. Packer, *Hot Tub Religion* (Wheaton, IL: Tyndale House, 1987), 91.

3. Fischer, *Growing Old in America*, 4.

4. Snyder, *In Pursuit of God*, 146.

Chapter 14. "The Cup is Half Empty" Syndrome

1. *St. Petersburg Times*, September 19, 2007, p. 5A.

Chapter 15. Breakdown in Relationships

1. Carol Dettoni, *Caring for Those Who Can't* (Wheaton, IL: Victor, 1993), 185.

2. Don Anderson, *Keep the Fire* (Sisters, OR: Multnomah Books, 1994), 288.

3. Dale Evans, *Time Out Ladies* (Westwood, NJ: Revell, 1974).

4. John MacArthur, *The Freedom and Power of Forgiveness* (Wheaton, IL: Crossway Books, 1998).

Chapter 16. Botox and Facelift Choices

1. "Turn Back the Clock" in *U.S. News and World Report*, 139.18, Nov. 14, 2005: 76.

2. Ibid, 77-78.

3. Frida Kerner Furman, *Facing the Mirror* (New York: Routledge, 1997), 93.

4. Charles Spurgeon, *Eccentric Preachers* (Pasadena, TX: Pilgrim Publications, 1978), 19.

5. Ibid, 29-30.

6. Furman, *Facing the Mirror*, 112-13.

7. Letty Cottin Pogrebin, *Getting Over Getting Older* (Boston: Little Brown, 1996), 149.

Chapter 17. Walking With the Lord

1. George E. Vaillant, *Aging Well* (Boston: Little Brown, 2002), 4.
2. Steve Seeman, "Die With Your Boots On," *Journey Magazine*, Winter 2005:33.
3. Arthur Bennett, ed. *The Valley of Vision* (Carlisle, PA: Banner of Truth Trust, 1995), 72.

Chapter 18. Maintaining Accountability

1. Vaillant, *Aging Well*, 215-218, 343.
2. John W. Rowe, M.D. and Robert L. Kahn, PhD., *Successful Aging* (New York: Random House, 1998), 213.

Chapter 19. Setting Specific Goals

1. Francis Schaeffer, *No Little People, No Little Places* (Downers Grove, IL: InterVarsity Press, 1974), 21-25; see also Luke 14:7-11.
2. Kenneth C. Fleming, *He Humbled Himself: Recovering the Lost Art of Serving* (Kansas City, KS: Walterick Publishers, 1989), 15-21.
3. Brother Lawrence, *The Practice of the Presence of God* (Westwood, NJ: Revell, 1958), 26.
4. Vaillant, *Aging Well*, 311.
5. Joseph D. Allison, *Setting Goals That Count* (Grand Rapids, MI: Chosen Books, 1985), 93-94.
6. Rick Pitino, *Success Is a Choice* (New York: Broadway Books, 1997), 47.
7. Ibid, 46.
8. David McNally, *The Eagle's Secret* (New York: Dell Publishing, 1990), 51.

Chapter 20. Choosing and Evaluating Activities

1. Rowe and Kahn, *Successful Aging*, 235.
2. Brother Lawrence, *The Practice of the Presence of God*, 27.
3. See also Psalm 119:89 and Isaiah 40:8.

Chapter 21. Dealing with Loss, Healing, and Disease

1. Rowe and Kahn, *Successful Aging*, 52.

2. Charles Swindoll, *Laugh Again* (Dallas, Word Publishing, 1992), 20.

3. Ibid. 201.

4. Judith Viorst, *Necessary Losses* (New York: Simon and Schuster, 1986), 285.

5. William Bates, *The Four Last Things: Death, Judgment, Heaven, Hell* (London: Printed for Brabazon Aylmer, at the Three Pigeons, against the Royal Exchange in Corhil, 1691), 19.

6. Ruth Lewshenia Kopp, M.D., *Encounter with Terminal Illness* (Grand Rapids, MI: Zondervan, 1980), 32

7. 2 Chronicles 16:12. Read Asa's interesting story in 2 Chronicles chapters 14-16.

8. One thinks, for example, of Joni Eareckson Tada, paraplegic author and speaker.

9. Ruth Lewshenia Kopp, M.D., *Encounter with Terminal Illness*, 55-56.

10. Ibid. 36.

11. J. C. Ryle, *Expository Thoughts on the Gospels* (Grand Rapids, MI: Zondervan. 2nd reprint ed., vols 3 and 4, 1957).

12. *The Psalms and Hymns of Isaac Watts* (Morgan, PA: Soli Deo Gloria Publ, 1997), 356.

13. For a similar problem verse see Psalm 91:10.

Chapter 22. "When My Trophies at Last I Lay Down"

1. Diane M. Komp, M.D., *A Window to Heaven* (Grand Rapids, MI: Zondervan, 1992), 28.

2. Billy Graham, *Facing Death* (Waco, TX: Word, 1987), 26.

3. Barbara Deane, *Caring for Your Aging Parents* (Colorado Springs, CO: NavPress, 1992), 223.

4. George Bennard, "The Old Rugged Cross," © 1913, renewed 1941. The Rodeheaver Co., a division of Word.

5. K. P. Yohannan, "What Keeps Us Going," in *Send* (Carollton, TX: Vol. 26, No 2), 23.

6. A. W. Tozer, *The Next Chapter After the Last* (Camp Hill, PA: Christian Publ, 1987), 6.

Suggested Reading

Baker, Don. *Heaven*. Portland, OR: Multnomah, 1983.

Clarkson, Margaret. *Destined for Glory: The Meaning of Suffering*. New York: Walker and Co, large print edition, by arrangement with Eerdmans, 1987.

Deane, Barbara. *Caring for Your Aging Parents*. Colorado Springs: NavPress, 1992.

Dettoni, Carol. *Caring for Those Who Can't*. Wheaton, IL: Victor, 1993.

Fischer, David Hackett. *Growing Old in America*. New York: Oxford UP, 1977.

Fleming, Kenneth C. *He Humbled Himself: Recovering the Lost Art of Serving*. Kansas City, KS: Walterick, 1989.

Gillick, Muriel R., M.D. *The Denial of Aging*. Cambridge: Harvard UP, 2006.

Graham, Billy. *Facing Death*. Waco, TX: Word, 1987.

Hamer, Gloria, *Help, Lord! I'm Hospitalized*. Grand Rapids: Daybreak Books, Zondervan, 1989.

Kopp, Ruth Lewshenia Kopp, M.D. *Encounter with Terminal Illness*, Grand Rapids: Zondervan, 1980.

Lewis, C. S. *A Grief Observed*. New York: Bantam Books, 1988.

Lewis, C. S. *The Problem of Pain*. New York: Macmillan, 1969.

Lutzer, Erwin, *One Minute After You Die*. Chicago: Moody Press, 1997.

MacArthur, John. *Anxious for Nothing: God's Cure for the Cares of Your Soul*. Colorado Springs, CO: Victor, 2006.

Robinson, Haddon. *Grief*. Grand Rapids: Discovery House, 1996.

Rowe, John W. M.D. and Kahn, Robert L. PhD. *Successful Aging*. New York: Random House, 1998.

Rushford, Patricia H. *Caring for Your Elderly Parents*. Grand Rapids: Revell, 1993.

Sipley, Richard M. *Understanding Divine Healing*. Wheaton, IL: Victor, 1986.

Smith, Olivia J. *Aging in America*. New York: H. W. Wilson, 2000.

Tada, Joni Eareckson. *When Is It Right to Die?* Grand Rapids: Zondervan, 1992.

Taylor, Franklin D., Sr. *Facing Death: Before and After*. Scarborough, ON, Canada: Everyday Publ, 1984.

Notes and Reflections